Sully's W[...]

Mick Sullivan – Rugby L[...]

Graham Williams

London League Publications Ltd

Sully's Way
Mick Sullivan – Rugby League Legend

© Graham Williams. Forewords © Billy Boston, Danny Lockwood. Introduction © Michelle Sullivan.

The moral right of Graham Williams to be identified as the author has been asserted.

Cover design © Stephen McCarthy.

Cover photos: Front: Mick playing for Great Britain on the 1958 tour (Courtesy *Rugby League Journal*); Mick wearing his first cap – NABC Rugby Union for England versus Wales; Back: Mick with his Hall of Fame medal and playing for Huddersfield against Bradford Northern.

All photographs are from private collections unless otherwise credited. No copyright has been intentionally breached; please contact London League Publications Ltd if you believe there has been a breach of copyright.

A CIP catalogue record for this book is available from the British Library.

First published in Great Britain in September 2015 by London League Publications Ltd, PO Box 65784, London NW2 9NS

ISBN: 978-1-909885-09-7

Cover design by Stephen McCarthy Graphic Design,
46, Clarence Road, London N15 5BB

Editing and layout by Peter Lush

Printed and bound in Great Britain by Charlesworth Press, Wakefield

Foreword: Billy Boston MBE

Mick Sullivan. A friend, team-mate and one of the toughest rugby league players I ever met.

My first meeting with Mick was in rugby union when England Boys Clubs met the Welsh Boys Clubs in Wales. I played for Cardiff Central Boys Clubs and I think Mick played for Shaw Cross Boys Club in Yorkshire at that time. We won that day, but I cannot remember the score. However, I do remember Mick as an extremely determined and committed player who feared noting and no one.

When Mick joined Wigan I was on the right wing and Sully, as he became known, played left wing. At that time it crossed my mind that I was very fortunate that he was now in our team and not in the opposition up against me on an opposing team's wing.

Sully and I became really good friends during his period at Wigan and also during our Lions tours.

I remember the match we played for the British Lions against New South Wales in 1962 at the Sydney Cricket Ground. Sully had been warned by our coach not be lured into any illegal rough play as he would be targeted. Second half and the Lions were winning. Next thing a bust up occurred on the left wing. Sully had thumped Michael Cleary, the Australian right winger. Ken Irvine, the Australian left winger and I sprinted over and tried to separate the two of them. The referee then sent Sully and Cleary for an early bath. Then to our astonishment he turned to Irvine and myself and said 'you two can follow them'. So that was four wing men in one game sent off. That was my first and only time I was sent off and all because of Sully.

The sad day came when Sully was transferred to St Helens. I missed his banter during training. The Christmas period loomed and we always played St Helens during that period each year. I did not fear his evil reputation as we were best friends. It was the second half. I cannot remember the score but all of a sudden I felt a sharp jab to might right jaw and next thing I looked up and there was Sully whistling and pretending it had nothing to do with him. Later in the bar I said to him "I thought we were best friends". His reply was "I hit friends as well Billy."

To this day I am proud to have Michael Sullivan as one of my very best friends from the game of rugby league,

Wigan
March 2015

Foreword: Danny Lockwood

The modern world is awash with 'stars' – superstars even – there being little differentiation between whether they have found their stardust in the world of music or sport, fashion or simply soap opera television. Glitz and glamour and artifice.

The world of rugby league has always managed to keep its feet on the ground, in touch with not just its fans but itself, better than most. But even in our sport, the 21st century professional is a revered individual, afforded courtesies, privileges and luxuries beyond the understanding of most of the people who, basically, pay his wage.

Wages. Actually, today they are salaries, contracts, future options and pension pots that the cast-iron men who created rugby league in the furnace of brutal competition could never have comprehended.

Fifty or so years ago – and far more recently in truth – that would have been a foreign language. Those men were less stars than they were heroes. Working class heroes. Daily, they rubbed industrial shoulders with the very men who come the weekend queued patiently, eagerly, at turnstiles through which they passed in order to witness the physical feats of rugby league players who asked, and gave, no quarter.

And come Monday, there they were again, back at work, no outward display of injury or physical impediment if it were at all possible. And no bravado either.

Among those many, many men of physical redoubt and skilled resource, there emerged rare individuals who transcended not just the ordinary, the good or the great, but who lit up generational imaginations of young and old alike.

A colossus on the park, a character off it. A man cut from a different cloth. Mick Sullivan was one such rugby league player, one such man.

The basic statistics of Mick Sully's remarkable career tell their own tale, as these following pages will in themselves reveal. I cannot however feel it isn't in some way perverse that a talent – a presence – like Michael Sullivan could be horse-traded between clubs for a sum approaching one million pounds in today's values, and yet be treated as nothing more than the hired help, a base commodity.

What would a player of Mick Sullivan's immense capabilities truly be worth today? It was a different age, in so many ways.

But what the directors and the fans of Huddersfield, Wigan and St Helens, and later York, his hometown Dewsbury and the friends he made on his Australian adventure always got, was nothing less than 100 per cent Sully. A lethal eye for the opposing tryline, matched – at the very least – by a ferocious and uncompromising lack of regard for his own physical safety. Skill, speed, strength and a desire to win that literally put the fear of God in opponents.

Defence as a form of attack? The modern Australians might like to think they invented the concept. Refined it perhaps – because there was never an opposing three-quarter who caught a ball and wasn't 'hearing footsteps' when Sully was timing an incursion.

He famously respected authority perhaps even less than he did his opponents – the 2013 induction to the RFL Hall of Fame was woefully belated for a man of his stellar record – but Sully was always a man at ease with himself, never happier than in the bosom of his family, or round a table with his many friends.

A man who played, lived and loved with everything he had, with a smile for all, and who left nothing behind in the changing rooms of life. Mick Sullivan.

Danny Lockwood is the Publisher of *League Weekly*

Acknowledgments

Sadly, due to his illness, Sully was unable to contribute to the preparation of his life story. Fortunately, his family have been very supportive, particularly his daughter Michelle who instigated the book and his brother Barry.

I would like to thank everyone who shared their memories of Sully with me, particularly David Smith, Norman Wainwright, Douglas Hird, Sam Morton, Ken Parratt, Margaret and Trevor Watson, Ray French, Alex Service and Austin Rhodes for giving me so much of their time to talk over past matches and times. I was also fortunate to be able to draw on John Musgrave's memories of their time together on National Service. The contributions of Billy Boston, Danny Lockwood and Mick Stevenson are greatly appreciated. Please accept my apologies if I have forgotten to mention anyone.

Mick Sullivan's May 2006 interview conducted by the National Archive of Rugby League Video Interviews was also particularly helpful. Tony Capstick, Trevor Delaney, Harry Edgar and Robert Gate provided valuable help and advice. Leeds Central Library's facilities have once again proved invaluable for research and the members of staff at the Rugby League Archive at Huddersfield University were also most helpful. The Saints Heritage Society website also proved very useful for checking details of Sully's later career. Earlier work done by members of the Rugby League Record Keepers' Club, in compiling its teams and scorers lists, provided further details of Sully's career.

Finally, thanks are due to Moira Doolan for her diligence in checking the text and helping to make it readable. Once again, thanks go to Peter Lush for not only getting this book underway but also for putting it together at the end.

I have tried to acknowledge the sources I have used, but if any copyrights have been infringed this is purely unintentional. Needless to say, any errors in the text are entirely my own responsibility.

Graham Williams

Introduction

It was just over a year ago that I decided I needed to do something that would help me deal with the illness my Dad has. After a lot of interest I decided that to have his biography written would not only help me in a lot of ways, but would also be a great tribute to my Dad.

I would like to thank Peter Lush who contacted me straight away and was very interested in London League Publications Ltd publishing this book and Graham Williams writing it.

I never realised what a challenge this would be and thought this could be done in about six months. Over a year later I find this has probably been the hardest thing I have ever done, both emotionally and mentally. As Dad was unable to have any input due to his illness this has had to be an authorised biography which as I have found out is so much harder to write and I have to thank Graham Williams for writing this on behalf of My Dad. Graham has been so patient carrying me along the way; the research he has done has been amazing and I am sure Dad would be very proud.

I would also like to thank everyone who has helped to make this possible with all the amazing appreciations, foreword and last word and also all the amazing stories I have come across from near and far. This has been a rollercoaster of emotions to see how Dad is still remembered and how much of a legend he was and still is.

As I am sure you will read, Dad was sometimes quite up front about a lot of things and I suppose on wanting to support his family and further his career abroad it led to a fall out with the RFL which to this Day I think was the reason behind Dad not ever getting the recognition he deserved, after all he did playing rugby for his country and everything he achieved along the way. For example, he only received a Great Britain cap by playing a full game, unlike today when a player only has to go on the pitch to earn one.

Dad to us will always be in our eyes 'Simply the best' as both a Dad and a rugby player. I could write thousands of words but that would not be enough to describe our Dad. As a rugby player he was known as a tough player and a record breaker. But also as our Dad he was a gentle giant and soft as putty, and a true gentleman off the pitch. Mum and Dad were married for 54 years and were true soul mates.

Although things were hard at times and Mum always said it was very lonely when Dad was away on tour, they always had each other. While Dad was away playing, Mum kept the family together. When Dad was on tour Mum would pack us up and take us back to Dewsbury to stay with her family for a while so she wasn't always on her own.

When Dad visited a different country he would always buy Mum a different gold charm for the bracelet he bought her. He also designed a pearl ring for her and had it made in South Africa so that there would be only one of its kind in the world. That is how much Mum meant to Dad. He would always buy her flowers most weeks, not just on birthdays and Valentine's Day, and present all the time – a real romantic really.

Their time in Australia was in their words the best time and they wished they had stayed there, because they had been made so welcome. As far as I know Dad is still an icon over there. Our time there as children was filled with adventure and happiness, we lived in the outback, which in itself is so different from life back in England.

Mum played tennis and we had a fantastic lifestyle. Mum and Dad had a great circle of friends who always said they could come back and visit and it would not cost them a penny. Mum and Dad always said they would return but unfortunately this never happened.

Off the pitch Dad was a true gentleman. He would help anyone and would always take time to sign autographs. He often gave his memorabilia away to fans and also to raise money for charity, particularly for Alzheimer's charities.

As a Dad he was the one who would let us get away with everything and when Mum said 'No', well off to Dad we would go and he would say 'Yes'. He was so soft, nothing like the hard man on the rugby pitch. During our time at Wigan, David used to hide in the back of Dad's car just before he would set off for training, that way he would end up training with the team; by the age of five he could kick a goal.

We were lucky enough to have had a great childhood, although we did move house a lot, we were lucky enough to live in Australia and to travel round the world on our return back to the UK. The memories we have, not only of our family life but of our Dad, who will always be a legend in our eyes, will last with us forever and we feel so lucky to have them.

Mum and Dad doted on their three grandchildren: Scott, Aimee and Mia and would take every opportunity to spend time with them. They used to take Scott on holiday to Scarborough, their favourite UK holiday destination and where they first met. Aimee would always stay with them in the school holidays and has so many memories of her time with Grandad and Grandma. Then Mia came along and was as spoilt as ever. Even though we live in York we saw Mum and Dad every week and they were always there whenever they were needed. Aimee was quite ill as a baby and when she was rushed into hospital, my Dad was there straight away. He had got the first train to York and was at the Hospital to give his support to me and his granddaughter.

I could go on forever about how much their grandchildren meant to them and also how much they meant to their grandchildren. As a Grandad he has been there for his grandchildren as both a Grandad and a father figure and they could not have asked for a better role model. Although they were all spoilt and in Grandad's eyes could do no wrong, they love and respect their Grandad to this day.

My Mum passed away on 1 July 2008 after a short illness which left us all devastated and to this day we still are. It was six months later, in January 2009, that Dad was diagnosed with Alzheimer's so not only were we dealing with Mum's death but now Dad's illness. After Dad deteriorated quite quickly, we were advised by the family doctor that he needed 24hour professional care which we couldn't give him so the decision was made that Dad would go into a care home so he could be looked after properly 24 hours a day.

Unfortunately Dad was then diagnosed with Prostrate Cancer as well, so he is not only fighting one illness but two. But true to form, he is still as tough as old boots. Dad is now in a nursing home in Snapethorpe in Wakefield where he is as happy as can be and is looked after very well. Alzheimer's is an awful illness for anyone to have and the day when they no longer know who you are is devastating. However, we have learnt to deal with this and as long as we get smiles from Dad that is all we need.

I have been helped so much by working on Dad's book. I think is was what I needed to help me come to terms with his illness. I know I will never have my Dad back as he used to be, but I have all these memories to look back on and cherish. I would also like to make a point that the specialist said to me when Dad was diagnosed with Alzheimer's that all the knocks his head had taken when playing rugby would probably have contributed to the onset of Alzheimer's. I know the Alzheimer's charity have been campaigning about this and I hope more can be done to prevent this and try and put measures in place to protect other sports men and women.

I would like to end this by saying Dad is special and unique, he never forgot his roots were he started his career, and he has always had respect for players and achievements for the greatest game in the World. Dad will always be **simply the best** and a **true legend** in our eyes.

Michelle Sullivan
York, April 2015

Thanks

London League Publications Ltd would like to thank Steve McCarthy for designing the cover, everyone who supplied photos – especially Harry Edgar at *Rugby League Journal* and Robert Gate – Paul McDermott and Dave Parker for their help in getting the book started, and the staff of Charlesworth Ltd for printing the book.

Peter Lush and Dave Farrar

Contents

1. The beginning	1
2. Huddersfield	13
3. The 1954 World Cup	17
4. The RAF and rugby union	27
5. League and union	31
6. For club and country	39
7. The 1957 World Cup	45
8. Moving on	49
9. The 1958 Lions tour	57
10. More success with Wigan	69
11. A World Cup and a transfer	81
12. The Kiwis and the Lancashire Cup	93
13. The 1962 Lions tour	101
14. A final season with Saints	111
15. York	117
16. Dewsbury and Junee	123
17. Coaching and beyond	131
18. Memories of Mick Sullivan	139
Appendix: Statistics and records	146

Note on values

We have not converted every financial value into its 2015 equivalent. To get an understanding of its likely equivalent a rough figure can be arrived at by multiplying the figure in the text by a factor of 20.

Abbreviations

FRL	French Rugby League	RFL	Rugby Football League
IB	International Board	YSC	Yorkshire Senior Competition
NRL	Northern Rugby League		

"The past is a foreign country: they do things differently there." (L.P. Hartley – *The Go-Between*)

Rugby league in Sully's playing time was very different from the sport that we know today.

The Northern Rugby League (NRL) was based exclusively in Cumberland, Lancashire and Yorkshire. For most of his playing career, there was one division, with teams having a fixture list primarily based on their own side of the Pennines. The Championship was settled by a play-off of the top four clubs, two semi-finals and the final.

As well as the NRL, there were County Leagues, based on the fixtures between teams in each county, with the two Cumberland clubs being in the Lancashire League, along with a Yorkshire club on occasions if the numbers were uneven. The County Cups were played for on a knock-out basis in the first part of the season. The only other competition was the Challenge Cup, which was the sport's most prominent tournament, and was played in the second half of the season culminating in the final at Wembley Stadium.

The game itself was also very different. For most of Sully's career, there were no substitutes, and if a team lost a player through injury they played a man short. Players generally stuck more rigidly to their positions than nowadays.

Scrums were competitive, and the main role of the hooker was to win the ball, often by any means necessary. There were unlimited tackles, unlike the six-tackle rule today. And the game was more physically challenging, although the players were all part-time, and only trained for two evenings a week.

Rugby union was still 'amateur' in Sully's time, and rugby league players – both amateur and professional – were banned from playing rugby union. Once a player had signed as a professional with a rugby league club, they were banned from playing rugby union.

However, when rugby league players were doing National Service, they were generally allowed to play rugby union for Forces teams, including in the prestigious inter-services matches. Rugby league was not played in the Armed Forces at this time.

Peter Lush

1. The beginning

Michael or 'Mick' Sullivan was an electrifying presence on the world's rugby league grounds for much of the 1950s and 1960s. Sully, as he was better known to his teammates, friends and fans was sometimes controversial, but always entertaining, over a long playing career that brought him practically every honour the game had to offer.

His story begins at the Hyde Park Maternity Home in Leeds on 12 January 1934. His father, Cyril, a millworker, hailed from Hunslet Carr, but had been living at Bankhouse in Pudsey for a month after taking a job at Lister's Mill in Troydale. Over the next few years the family grew, with first another son, Barry, and then a daughter, Margaret. Michael attended the nearby Littlemoor Infants School, Greenside Junior School and finally Littlemoor Secondary Modern, where he started just as World War Two was drawing abruptly to a close in the Far East. Sully was good at all sports, but at secondary school was an enthusiastic cricketer and footballer. He regularly attended at Pudsey Parish Church where he and his brother sang in the choir.

Home was on the edge of the Fulneck Valley and Sully enjoyed the freedoms it provided. There was space and time to roam as well as more essential tasks such as rabbiting and collecting windfall apples to supplement the family's wartime diet. While Pudsey suffered only one direct air raid, the anti-aircraft batteries on the edge of the town ensured that no one was unaware that its location, between Leeds and Bradford, meant there was always a possibility of the sirens sounding, causing the family to evacuate to the relative safety of the Anderson shelter.

At the age of 14, Sully passed the examination to earn a scholarship to study full-time at Dewsbury Technical College. It was an arduous daily bus journey, but would prove well worth it. He did not realise at the time that the course in Dewsbury would change the entire course of his young life. As his soon to be best friend David Smith remembers: "My first meeting with Michael was in April 1948, when we became classmates at Dewsbury Technical School. We were both members of the latest intake of students taking a two year course in Basic Building Studies, which were known as B1 and B2. Being seated next to Michael we quickly became best friends. I discovered that Michael lived in Pudsey and had to make the one hour bus trip to Dewsbury every morning and the same return journey in the evening. He was older than the majority of the class who were mostly 13 years old. Michael was 14 years old and this age difference had a sporting impact on him during his second year at the Tech."

"Going back a few months to the start of 1947–48 local rugby league season, I had joined the newly formed Shaw Cross boys club, and was appointed the first captain of the under–16 team. As a newly formed club, we found the going hard, losing most of our matches by big scores, the largest being an 84–0 defeat by Batley Boys. The bad results had a knock-on effect, many of the team dropped out and we struggled most games to field a full team. However, we got to the last match of the season, in May 1948, which was a midweek evening game against the local YMCA team."

"As had become the norm at this time, we were struggling to raise a team, so I mentioned to my new best mate, Michael, did he fancy helping us out and playing for us. He told me he had never played rugby league and didn't know anything about it. Now, my usual position was stand-off but I said to Michael that he could play on the wing and I would play centre to him, that way I could talk him through the positioning etc, so he agreed to play for us."

"Overlooking the town of Dewsbury there is a large stretch of hillside known locally as Caulms Wood, although in 1948 there were very few trees to be seen. During the war the Army had built a camp there where they had positioned large guns to protect the local area from enemy warplanes. When the war finished the local council took the area over, the billets were used to house homeless people, while the field where the guns were situated was turned into a playing area. It was on this field that Michael played his first game. During that first season at Shaw Cross I and my team mates had become used to changing for matches in some strange places; in garages, Sunday Schools, pit baths and behind walls to name but a few. But even I was surprised when we were led to one of the camp billets and taken into a small bedroom and told to get changed in there, around the occupier's bed. I don't know what Michael thought he had let himself in for."

"So he played his first game, didn't have a lot to do, mainly defence as we went down to yet another heavy defeat. But he did show enough promise to make a useful asset to our team for the next season."

"That night he stayed overnight at my home and this became a regular event, mostly at weekends. My father, Harry V. Smith, was the secretary of the local amateur Rugby League and quickly saw the raw talent that Michael possessed. Every Sunday morning we would be out in the local park training and this carried on until Michael signed for Huddersfield in May 1952."

"When the new season arrived in September 1948, Michael and I had been busy during the close season and had persuaded several of our school mates and friends to join us at Shaw Cross and it quickly became apparent that we were a good side. Also it was soon clear that on our wing we had someone special. When Michael got the ball he was virtually unstoppable. He was lightening fast, with a huge side-step and swerve. In his first season he scored over 30 tries and earned the nickname of the 'Pudsey Flier' which stuck with him throughout his amateur career."

"Michael was now staying at my home most Tuesday and Thursday evenings and also at the weekends. During the summer months when we went on holiday, Michael came long too, when we went to Scarborough. During the summer most of the textile and woollen mills would close for a fortnight, being locally known as Dewsbury feast week, which occurred on the last full week in July and also the following week. So many of the local people used to make their way to the coast for a holiday, Scarborough being our chosen favourite, they would meet up on the sands each day. Among the people we used to meet up with was a family called Hopkins, who had a daughter called Jean. Jean and Michael took a fancy to one another and started going out together. Jean later went on several family holidays with us and then later became Michael's wife."

"During our second term at the Tech, we persuaded our sports teacher to form a rugby league team. His name was Dennis Evans, who at the time was playing for the [professional] Dewsbury Rugby League team. We had a very successful season. We won the local schools' trophy and suffered only one defeat all season. Unfortunately, Michael was not able to play for the team due to him being too old to qualify, but nevertheless he supported the team in all our games."

"Michael's career went from strength-to-strength at Shaw Cross. He played regularly for the local league's town team, Yorkshire at various age groups and also England, again at different age groups.

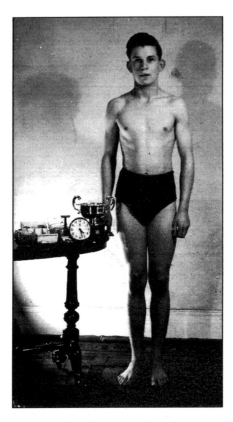

Left: Mick with his swimming trophies.

Below: Shaw Cross Boys Club rugby league team.

In the 1951–52 season, the Huddersfield Rugby League club signed Michael as an amateur player, but he still played the occasional game at Shaw Cross and with the local town team. He also played in amateur representative games."

Shaw Cross Boys' Club

Formed by a dozen teenagers in the austere aftermath of the Second World War, the Shaw Cross Boys' Club took its name from Shaw Cross village, which lies on the Leeds Road to the north of Dewsbury. Back in 1947, Shaw Cross had nothing for its youth to do and so that small group, most of whom had attended the same school and taken classes at the Dewsbury and Batley Tech, decided to organise something for themselves. They had no money, no pitch and no premises, but more than enough enthusiasm to get things moving. Having formed a rugby league club, the Dewsbury and Batley Amateur League offered them fixtures and the boys were on their way.

Lying in the shadow of the Shaw Cross Colliery, the club quickly unearthed and nurtured a tremendous seam of sporting interest and support. Dewsbury Corporation gave permission for the boys to prepare their own pitch on the village's recreation ground. An old Nissen hut, acquired from a former Army camp, was re-erected by the boys as a club house. All their sterling efforts were coming to fruition when Sully arrived on the scene in the spring of 1948.

Rugby league was the most popular choice for the lads and they turned out to be a talented bunch. The club ran teams at under–16, under–18 and finally at under–21 level in competitions held under the auspices of the Dewsbury and Batley ARL. Sully's first taste of success came as a member of the club's under–16 team, which won the Heavy Woollen District Junior Cup in 1949–50.

Training sessions were well organised and held on Tuesday and Thursday evenings, generally starting on a floodlit car park and ending with some road running to build stamina. Usually when training was over, Sully and Norman Wainwright would practice with the ball, playing touch-and-pass under the streetlights on Leeds Road.

As Douglas Hird and Alan Lancaster explain in their history of the club, Mick "trained hard, he was usually the first to arrive for training and the last to leave, and it was soon evident that this 10 stone lad would be a 'star' of tomorrow. He represented the club in athletics and swimming, winning prizes for both and soon became an inter-league player, a county representative and then an England RL junior."

At the insistence of his father, after leaving the Technical College where he had been Head Boy in his second year, Sully went looking for an apprenticeship. His two years of study behind him, Sully was taken on by a local plumbing firm based in the Chapeltown district of Pudsey.

While Shaw Cross was filling most of his winter months, Sully was not lost completely to his home town's sporting pursuits. It was a town with a much-prized cricketing reputation and Sully enjoyed spending some of his summers playing cricket at Pudsey St Lawrence. A non-smoker and teetotaller, Sully also trained in the summer with the Bramley Harriers which meant he maintained his fitness all year round.

1950–51

This season marked the start of Sully's rapid rise to the top flight. By the end of it, the Shaw Cross Boys' Club team had won through to play in the Yorkshire under–21 final. Sully was still only aged 16 and there were concerns for his safety in much older company, but he was so fast and strong that it was decided he could not really be left out. He was picked and travelled with the team over to York to play the York based Imperial Athletic on Saturday 14 April.

It was the Shaw Cross club's first appearance in a major final and appearing alongside Sully was another future test regular, Derek Turner, and five other players – Peter Blackburn (Dewsbury), Alan Lancaster (Bradford Northern, Huddersfield, Doncaster), Allen Lockwood (Dewsbury, Hull KR, Leeds), Peter Oldroyd (Rochdale Hornets) and Norman Wainwright (Huddersfield, Batley) – who would later play professionally.

The match did not go to plan for the visitors. Norman Wainwright, the captain, and Allen Lockwood were both dismissed and 'Pinky' Smith suffered a broken ankle. Short of three players, Shaw Cross did well to only lose 12–3.

'Pinky' Smith's injury meant he was unable to work. With no money coming in, York Imperial agreed to play a charity match for his benefit. The match was played on the school pitch at Thornhill Lees. Among the crowd on the touchline were a couple of well-dressed men – Bill

Cunningham and J. Wood-Beaver – who were members of the Huddersfield RLFC's committee. They liked what they saw and soon were putting plans together for Shaw Cross's talented young left wing pairing of Wainwright and Sully to join their squad at Fartown.

NABC

Youth had its advantages and it brought Sully plenty of opportunities to play lots of sport. The Shaw Cross club was affiliated to both the National Association of Boys Clubs and its Yorkshire County Association. That provided Sully with the opportunity to swim competitively for the club and to win both the 100 yards and 220 yards at the Yorkshire Association sports.

When requested by the County Association, the club forwarded the names of a number of its young rugby players for consideration by the selectors who were choosing an English rugby union team to play their Welsh counterparts. This opportunity was only possible because the RFU did not consider anyone who played rugby league to be a professional before their 18th birthday.

Shortly after arriving for training one evening, Norman Wainwright and Sully were called over and told that they had been selected to play for England at rugby union, a game they had never played. The pair would be playing centre and right wing for a National Association of Boys Clubs under–18 England team against a Welsh team at The Gnoll in Neath on 18 November 1950.

There was at least one familiar face to turn to for support on the day because Harry Smith attached himself to the team as an unofficial trainer, but coaching was minimal. Norman can only remember being told to release the ball when tackled and palm it away. Norman's centre partner was Geoff Palmer, the future Halifax rugby league centre, who was playing for Maryport Boys Club at the time. Despite the unfamiliarity of the rules, Sully managed to score a try in a narrow 8–6 defeat.

Norman and Sully were also selected for the return match at the Memorial Ground in Bristol on 28 April 1951. Sully scored two tries against a Welsh team that was captained by Billy Boston. Joe Erskine, like Boston representing Cardiff Central Boys Club, played stand-off for the Welsh team. He later embarked on a successful boxing career,

7

which saw him become the British Heavyweight champion. Included in the Welsh pack was Don Devereux, from Neath YMCA Boys' Club, who would later switch to rugby league with Huddersfield.

Three Shaw Cross boys appeared in the English Boys' Clubs team for the match against Wales the following season – Austin Kilroy and David Smith were the centres and Sully was again on the right wing. Also in the team for the match at Neath on Saturday 23 February 1952 was John Barton from Wigan Boys Club, the future Leigh and Wigan rugby league forward. Billy Boston, the Welsh captain, proved too powerful for the English boys and at half-time Wales led 19–0. Not long after play resumed, Austin Kilroy suffered a broken collarbone. When the final whistle came, the Welsh had thrashed the short-handed English Boys 32–0.

By the time the next match came around, Sully had passed his 18th birthday and that appeared to have ended his rugby union days forever. Sully may have grown too old for the world of rugby union, but the Shaw Cross Club would continue to provide boys for NABC XV's for some time to come.

1951–52

It had been expected that Norman Wainwright would sign for Batley and a number of professional clubs were said to be interested in Sully, with Hunslet, the club he supported as a boy, thought to be the favourite. Neither forecast proved to be correct. Norman Wainwright signed professional forms for Huddersfield on 6 September, while because of his age Sully could only sign as an amateur. Sully would collect just his expenses playing for Huddersfield's 'A' team in 1951–52. Over the season, Sully made 25 appearances and scored 23 tries for the 'A' team. His best haul coming against newcomers to the professional game Doncaster, on 13 October, when he scored four tries in a 60–0 win. The 'A' team went on to finish as the runner up in both the YSC and in the YSC Challenge Cup.

After appearing in a County trial, Sully was called up to play for Yorkshire in the Amateur County Championship against Lancashire at Halifax and Cumberland at Whitehaven. It was a sign of how highly Sully was rated that he was picked for the England amateur international open age team this season. Brought forward from its usual Easter date at the request of the BBC, the meeting with France was scheduled to be played at Bradford Northern's Odsal Stadium on the evening of Tuesday 5 February. When Odsal's pitch was declared unfit, the RFL began an urgent search for an alternative ground with floodlights. Odsal was the only rugby league grounds with floodlights at this time. Manchester United agreed that the club's training ground, The Cliff in Broughton, could be used. The pitch was ready for the match to go ahead two days later than scheduled. Whether the Cliff's floodlights would have been powerful enough was never tested because the BBC had by then decided that it would have to cancel the live broadcast so Sully, who appeared on the right wing, missed his first chance to appear on television. A dour match, which ended in a 3–3 draw, saw the English avoid defeat at the hands of the French for the first time since the war.

Two months later, Sully made the first of his two appearances in the England under–21 team, which in those days featured a mixture of amateur and professional players. It was a strong squad that in addition to Sully included five other players – Frank Collier, Laurie Gilfedder, Geoff Gunney, Don Metcalfe and Jeff Stevenson – who would go on to win senior international honours. However, on their home soil at Avignon the French proved too strong winning 10–7.

A good first season over, Sully signed professional forms for Huddersfield on 29 May 1952. When he signed, Sully was described as a light, but very fast, winger, who was able to swerve and side-step without losing pace. He was obviously a very highly rated young man and with the help and advice of Harry Smith secured a very good contract. Huddersfield's secretary, Arthur Archbell, paid him a signing on fee of £500, enough to buy a substantial terraced house. There was also the option of a further £500 if Sully would sign a further contract in five years time. If not, he would be allowed a free transfer. Additional payments of £50 for his first Yorkshire appearance and £100 for international honours would also be made. In addition, Shaw Cross Boys Club received a payment of £50 of which £10 went to the Batley and Dewsbury ARL.

Professional rugby league was a part-time game in those days and there was no guaranteed wage, weekly or monthly, on offer. Match payments were provided by contract and while in the 'A' team Sully would receive £6 for a win and £4 for a defeat. When promoted to the first team, he would receive £8 for an away win and £6 for a home win. There was the possibility for additional bonuses for big matches, but there would be no payments in the close season, only expenses for attendance at training and an insurance payment in the case of injury.

These terms were very generous and certainly better than those offered to most rugby league juniors. However, Sully's overall income would depend on how well the team played and any loss of form would mean a drop in the cash received. Playing and hopefully winning twice a week in the early or late season would bring good money, but a day job, while not mandatory, was necessary to make up the weekly income. Sully would continue as an apprentice on £2/10 (£2.50) a week and attend technical college on three nights a week in Leeds where he would study towards his City and Guilds exams.

A very understanding employer was essential as time off would be needed for midweek afternoon matches, midweek evening training sessions and often on Saturday mornings, then still part of the normal working week, when the match was a significant distance away. Even with a very sympathetic employer, it was not always an easy relationship and Sully would have to learn to juggle the demands of all those who wanted his services. Sully was one of many players who found it a not always rewarding struggle.

Leaving the amateur ranks in rugby league meant the loss of his amateur status in other sports and it meant that Sully, who revelled in the sporting life, was forced to give up some of his most enjoyable pastimes. He was immediately barred from taking part in amateur swimming competitions and the local water polo leagues that he had enjoyed as a member of Pudsey Swimming Club. He also had to cease his involvement with Bramley and District Harriers.

1950 National Association of Boys Clubs Rugby Union team.

Norman Wainwright and Mick wearing their NABC caps.

Playing for Huddersfield in 1954.
(Photo: Courtesy *Rugby League Journal*)

2. Huddersfield

The club that Sully joined had been one of the strongest in post-war rugby league and was noted throughout the north for producing high class football. To provide football of that class, the members of the first-team had been recruited from all parts of the British Isles and the Antipodes. It was a well balanced team that had enabled Huddersfield to make a serious challenge for the top honours each year since the war; the Championship and the Yorkshire League had been won in 1947–48, the Yorkshire Cup in 1949–50 and 1950–51 and the Yorkshire League in 1951–52.

At Fartown, Sully came under the overall control of Bill Smith, the club's veteran Welsh trainer. When his playing career which included spells with Batley, Bradford Northern and Castleford ended, Bill Smith briefly became Batley's trainer before moving on to Headingley where he prepared the 1936 Leeds Challenge Cup Final team. He returned to Batley as trainer during the war years before taking over at Fartown in 1951. Smith provided the disciplined training environment Sully relished and also helped him work on his sprinting.

1952–53

Sully was still primarily learning his trade in the 'A' team. He made 21 appearances, scoring 21 tries, for the 'A' team, which finished in fourth place in the YSC.

He made his first-team debut for Huddersfield against Dewsbury at Crown Flatt on Saturday 4 October, when he deputised for Australian winger Lionel Cooper. He was again called up to deputise for Cooper, who was required by Other Nationalities for an International Championship match, in a Yorkshire Cup semi-final replay at Halifax's Thrum Hall on 16 October. Sully scored a try towards the end of the first half to give 'Fartown' a 7–3 lead. Huddersfield progressed through to the final, where they beat Batley at Headingley, but Sully was not required on the big day.

The following Saturday he was back in the first-team at York, once more because Cooper was absent on Other Nationalities' duties. Sully was only occasionally called upon to play in the first team in the New Year. They were having a great season and by beating Wigan at Odsal

13

Stadium at the end of March in the Challenge Cup semi-final earned a trip to Wembley for the first time in 20 years.

Success in a second cup competition meant April was a busy month. There were eight league fixtures to complete, with a possible top-four finish on the cards, and an appearance at Wembley. Sully was called up to stand in for Lionel Cooper, again wanted by Other Nationalities, at Headingley on Saturday 11 April. He was not required for the next two Saturdays, when the final team was given a run out against Wigan ahead of the big day.

Huddersfield had tremendous strength in depth in the backs at this time. For Wembley, Huddersfield's threequarter line included two Australian internationals – Pat Devery and Lionel Cooper – on the left wing while the right wing pairing comprised a rugby union All Black – Peter Henderson – and an English rugby league international – Russ Pepperell. The club could afford to leave out Dick Cracknell, who had won two caps on Great Britain's right wing against the Kiwis in 1951. Cracknell's absence did not affect Huddersfield and they went on to beat St Helens 15–10 in a thrilling final.

Four days later, Sully was brought into the Huddersfield team that met Castleford in a league match at Fartown. He helped himself to two tries in an easy win, 38–5, that cemented the home team's claim to fourth place in the NRL and a place in the end of season play-offs that decided the Championship.

That was the end of the regular season for Sully. He had made a total of 10 first team appearances, one of them a friendly. In his nine league and cup fixtures, he had accumulated a very creditable seven tries.

Unusually, there were more friendlies still to come. A summer tournament, held in conjunction with the local council during the town's annual sports week, was staged on Stanley Park Oval for the Blackpool Corporation Challenge Cup in the early 1950s. Huddersfield was one of the four entrants this year and Sully enjoyed a couple of days on the Fylde coast, although victory in the final went to Barrow.

1953–54

Sully once again enjoyed a good 'A' team season. He made 28 appearances and scored a record 30 tries – six against Hunslet at

Fartown on 31 October. Although the reserve team could only repeat its fourth place finish in the YSC, they did provide Sully with his first honour as a professional. He was a member of the victorious Huddersfield 'A' team that beat Hull 'A' in the final of the Yorkshire Senior Cup. Despite being played in torrential rain on a midweek evening, 14 May, the final attracted a large crowd to Fartown, where the home team won comfortably 26–3. Sully wound up his 'A' team commitments with an appearance in an end-of-season friendly.

Even though Dick Cracknell was transferred to Oldham in October, first team opportunities were few. Like the previous season, when they did first start to come, in early October, it was because of Lionel Cooper's Other Nationalities' commitments. There were a further three matches in the New Year, but altogether Sully played in only five league and cup first team matches, scoring just one try.

Sully was selected for a second appearance for the England under–21 side, once again at Avignon. Although by now a professional, Sully received no payment beyond expenses for this match. Fortunately for Sully, the days of travelling to France by train and boat were over. Now, teams travelled by air from Blackbushe Airport near Camberley in Surrey to Avignon. Flying in a Douglas Dakota DC3 was hardly luxurious, but at least it was much quicker journey.

Once again the selectors fielded a strong team, which included future full internationals, Jim Challinor, Don Fox, Ike Southward and Geoff Gunney. This time they had the measure of the French. Sully had the satisfaction of scoring a try as the English managed to get back into winning ways after losing the two previous encounters with the French.

1954–55

One year on, Huddersfield's Wembley winning team was beginning to break up. Over the close season, a number of major players announced their retirement; most notably the team's veteran hooker, George Curran, the club's captain at Wembley, Russ Pepperell, and his centre partner, Pat Devery, who was the first of the club's Australian trio to decide to return home.

There were opportunities opening up for Sully who was earmarked to fill Pat Devery's place in the first-team. Sully's left-wing partner and mentor was the great Australian, Lionel Cooper, and he paid him this compliment some years later in *This is Rugby League:* "I played centre to Cooper in my first year as a professional at Huddersfield and couldn't have asked for better partner to show me the art of wing play for when I eventually moved to the flank."

Sully took over the left centre position for the usual pre-season friendly against Halifax and rapidly made it his own. By the end of September, Huddersfield had played eight league and three Yorkshire Cup matches of which seven had been won. At a time of change, the club's management must have been very pleased that the new left-wing pairing was showing real promise – Sully having scored six tries so far while his wing partner, Lionel Cooper, had already recorded an impressive 21 tries on his own account.

3. The 1954 World Cup

A new departure on the international scene was about to provide exciting opportunities for the game as a whole and Sully in particular. The FRL's long campaign for a World Cup tournament had finally come to fruition. Scheduled shortly after Great Britain's 1954 tour of Australasia, the first World Cup tournament presented the RFL with major selection problems. Reports on the indiscipline that had marred the tour both on and off the field were considered by the Rugby League Council at a meeting in Manchester on 13 September. Following the Council's deliberations, it was announced that six unnamed players had been blacklisted.

The handling of the tour report led to significant bad feeling and 10 of the tourists declared themselves unavailable for the tournament. One of those players to declare himself unavailable was Oldham's Terry O'Grady, the incumbent left winger. Although a year younger than Sully, O'Grady had made five test appearances on the summer tour and was probably looking forward to a longish tenure.

A further 13 players did likewise, although whether this was in protest over the RL Council's actions or, as is more likely, over difficulties in getting time off work or the poor terms on offer, is not clear. For three weeks away from work in France the players were offered £25 plus a £10 bonus if they won the tournament, which did not compare well to their club terms.

However, once the tournament was underway, James Hilton, the RFL chairman, said that if Great Britain finished as winners the Council might improve those terms. Subsequently the winning bonus was improved to £25.

Denied the services of so many experienced players, the 18 man squad, when announced on Thursday 30 September, was bound to be a relatively inexperienced party. In the end it contained only three members of the Australasian tour party – Gerry Helme (Warrington), Phil Jackson (Barrow) and Dave Valentine (Huddersfield). Another tourist, Willie Horne, was selected, but turned down the opportunity to play, which meant that the captaincy passed to Dave Valentine.

Just 20 years old, Sully was very much a surprise choice. As he told Ray French in *Match of my Life:* "I never expected to be selected. I was merely a kid who had just broken into the Huddersfield side, playing centre to the great Lionel Cooper. I hadn't even played for Yorkshire. I was plucked from nowhere. Everyone said I wasn't big enough or good enough, but I knew I could tackle and I had confidence in myself."

Sully had gone from being a promising youngster to an international player in one jump, for which he would receive the £100 he was entitled to under the terms of his Huddersfield contract.

When Halifax's Alvin Ackerley was unable to get three weeks off work, Sully' club team-mate Harry Bradshaw was brought into the party, which now included five from Fartown – Billy Banks, Harry Bradshaw, Ron Rylance, Mike Sullivan and Dave Valentine.

Most commentators wrote off the party's chances of success in France. However, the RFL's International and Selection Committee decided that some special training sessions were called for to help Great Britain deal with the challenge of a tournament that was scheduled to run from 30 October to 13 November. To run the sessions, the committee decided on Thursday 7 October to bring in Leigh's Joe Egan, a former fixture in the test pack as a player, who was in the process of building a new reputation for himself as a coach.

Egan organised two afternoon training sessions, the first at Rochdale on Wednesday 13 October and the second at Huddersfield one week later. Having tried to get the squad into some shape over the three weeks prior to departure, Egan was informed that his presence was no longer required. Responsibility for the team's performance from then onwards lay with the captain, Dave Valentine.

Having appeared in all Huddersfield's matches that season during which he had scored had eight tries, it was time for Sully to turn his back on club rugby and take his place on the international stage. The Yorkshire members of the party met up early in Huddersfield before making their way over to Manchester where they joined up with the rest of the squad on Monday 25 October. It was an early start; they left at 9am for the long road trip to Dover, then a night ferry crossing before arriving in Paris late the following afternoon.

Six days later, Sully made his test debut at centre against Australia, the favourites for the competition, at Lyon on Sunday 31 October 1954. A heavy tackle by his opposite number, Harry Wells left Sully with a badly cut eyebrow. These were the days before substitutes, when an injured player went off the field his team mates had to continue without him.

The 1954 Great Britain World Cup squad in Leeds on their way
to France. (Photo: Courtesy Robert Gate)

Gideon Shaw with the Great Britain players in a training session
at Huddersfield before the tournament.
(Photo: Courtesy *Rugby League Journal*)

19

Although his team manager, Castleford's Gideon Shaw, told Sully he could stay off because his eyelid had dropped below his eye, he bravely returned after having it taped back.

While he was off the field having his wound stitched, Dave Valentine dropped back to fill in at centre. Just seconds before half-time, Valentine made a break and fed Frank Kitchen who ran 60 yards for a try. Jimmy Ledgard converted to send Britain in at the break 12–5 ahead. Sully was back on the field after the break when the Lions extended their lead to 28–5. The Aussies could not close the gap and the Lions had a surprise 28–13 win.

That night the Lions celebrated long and hard in a Lyon bistro. For the first time the impossible dream looked like it might become a reality. It was lucky they had a full week off as the coach journey from Lyon to Toulouse took a gruelling 13 hours.

Although there was some doubt about the cut over his eye healing sufficiently, Sully was moved onto the left wing to replace the injured Frank Kitchen against France at Toulouse. The French were a major force on the international stage at this time and a record attendance created an intimidating atmosphere in the stadium. It was a very hard match between two teams very evenly matched. In the end the honours finished even, in a 13–13 draw.

The British backline was again reshuffled for the third match against New Zealand at Bordeaux on Armistice Day, which was a public holiday in France. Sully returned to left centre in place of Warrington's Ally Naughton and Frank Kitchen was recalled on the left wing.

An injury-stricken Kiwi team offered very little threat to Great Britain. The Lions gained the advantage and slowly built their lead. Unfortunately for the Lions, Frank Kitchen's leg injury forced him to leave the field in the second half. His absence did not undermine the Lions' performance who hung on to win comfortably 26–6.

Victory over the Kiwis meant that both France and Great Britain had finished with the same record – two wins and a draw. Although both had the same number of points, the Lions were on top of the final table due to a slightly superior scoring record. The tournament's organisers decided that a play-off between the two countries was needed to decide which nation should be crowned world champion. So instead of heading straight for home from Bordeaux, the British coach driver had to make a hastily arranged detour to Paris for an additional match.

Frank Kitchen's injury did not respond to treatment quickly enough, so Sully was chosen on the wing once more against France in the play-off held at the Parc des Princes in Paris on Saturday 13 November. Great Britain's team that day was: Jim Ledgard (Leigh), David Rose (Leeds), Phil Jackson (Barrow), Albert Naughton (Warrington), Mick Sullivan (Huddersfield), Gordon Brown (Leeds), Gerry Helme (Warrington), John Thorley (Halifax), Stan Smith (Hunslet), Bob Coverdale (Hull), Don Robinson (Wakefield Trinity), Basil Watts (York), David Valentine (Huddersfield).

In fine weather, a hugely partisan crowd of 30,368 was there to cheer on the home side. Those British fans that were fortunate to have access to a television set were able to sit and watch the whole of the match, which was broadcast live by the BBC through the new Eurovision link.

As anticipated, it was a hard fought, exciting contest. Great Britain turned round 6–2 ahead, but the French struck back to lead 9–6. It was a vital stage in the match and Great Britain had to regain the initiative. Securing possession from a ruck near the French line, Gerry Helme broke away and it looked certain that he would put Sully in for his first try of the tournament. However, as he did so often, Helme had thrown the perfect dummy and grabbed the opportunity to score himself. That try was converted, as was another by Gordon Brown to build a vital lead. The French struck back again and closed to within four points with 20 minutes left. The French could not reduce the margin any further and the unrated team had secured the world crown for Great Britain.

He might have played in all four matches, but Sully would have been disappointed to be the only Great Britain threequarter not to have scored a try. As soon as the tournament celebrations were over, the players boarded the coach for Manchester. On arrival, there was no official reception for the unexpected world champions. They went their separate ways; Sully and his teammates caught a train to Huddersfield. Later, each player received a blazer badge through the post.

His first taste of life on the international stage over, Sully and his four teammates were back in the Huddersfield team that travelled to Leigh on Saturday 20 November. The team returned defeated, but Sully went on to collect winning pay from home and away wins over Wakefield Trinity and a home win over Bradford Northern.

Mick tackling one of the New Zealanders during the 1954 World Cup.
(Photo: Courtesy Robert Gate)

Then, just over a month after that marvellous victory in France, there was another big day that would keep Sully out of the Huddersfield first team. On Saturday 18 December Mick was otherwise engaged, getting married to Jean at Dewsbury Parish Church. Many of his teammates were there to wish the young couple well, but then had to dash away to Fartown for the match against Leigh. For them there was no happy ending because Huddersfield lost 20–14, after leading at half-time.

Unlike most young couples at this time, Jean and Mick did not have to move in with either of their parents. They were able to start married life in their own home on Ernest Jones Street in Dewsbury. After a short honeymoon in Blackpool, Sully was back to take his place in the first team for the visit on Christmas Day of Halifax. It was a day to forget at Fartown because Halifax won 15–0.

Immediately after the Christmas holidays, Huddersfield went into the market transfer market and signed George Roughley, a centre, from Salford as cover for Sully, who it was said was due to join the Armed Forces for his National Service.

The 1954 Great Britain World Cup winners.
(Photo: Courtesy *Rugby League Journal*)

Mick receiving his Great Britain cap from legendary Huddersfield winger Albert
Rosenfeld in 1954. Dave Valentine looks on at them and the World Cup.
(Photo: Courtesy Robert Gate)

Mick and Jean's Wedding

Mick and Jean sign the register on their Wedding Day, 18 December 1954, as Mick's mother, Jean's parents and the Vicar look on.

Norman Wainwright, Lionel Cooper, Johnny Hunter and Dave Valentine congratulate Mick and Jean.

The happy couple

Mick and Jean with family members and bridesmaids.

Cutting the cake, which had been made by Norman Wainwright.
The lower tier has a rugby pitch on it.

26

4. The RAF and rugby union

Now aged 21, Sully's call up could no longer be deferred and National Service loomed. As far as Mick was concerned, he was destined for the Army, but when he confirmed he could be interested in joining the RAF, RFL Secretary Bill Fallowfield passed on his name to wing commander Neil Cameron, the secretary of the RAF Rugby Union.

Since being appointed as the Union's secretary in 1952, Cameron had worked hard to build links with the RFL and its member clubs. Even though he was now a professional rugby league player, Sully was able to play rugby union once more because the RFU waived its rules over professionalism for players doing National Service. Rugby league was not played in the Armed Forces at this time.

Cameron quickly blocked the Army's interest in young Sully and expedited his path into the Air Force. While Sully's interest in becoming a Physical Training Instructor, a role many professional sportsmen had done during the Second World War, was not possible as a National Serviceman, Cameron wrote directly making the following suggestion: "Your first aim is to get your rugby with Huddersfield on the Saturday and we will devise some sort of interesting job for you in the meantime. The main object (I think you will agree) is to get you stationed in or around Huddersfield and what you do when you come into the RAF is of secondary importance, though important nevertheless."

There was a last chance to say farewell to civilian life and Sully took it in style, running in two tries in a 32–15 win over Hull at Fartown on Saturday 29 January 1955. With his training rank of Aircraftman, Sully began two years of National Service at the RAF's huge kitting out camp at Cardington near Bedford on the following Monday. Having spent nearly a week there, during which he had been given a forces' haircut and received all the necessary kit and inoculations, Sully then moved onto RAF West Kirby on the Wirral. There he completed his eight weeks of basic training as part of the Trenchard squad. For his efforts in defence of the nation Sully would, like all the rest of the intake, receive the princely sum of £1/8 (£1.40) per week.

For most of the intake there was the frustration of being confined to camp until basic training had made them a credit to the uniform. But, Sully, like every other prominent athlete, was never bound by the same set of rules and regulations as the rest of the recruits. When he reported, Sully was already aware that only 48 hours after joining up he would be thrown straight into the RAF team to play Cambridge University, even though the RAF XV had already played a few matches that season.

Ten days later, on Saturday 12 February, Sully was one of three rugby league professionals chosen to play against the Royal Navy at Twickenham in a prestigious inter-services fixture. The other two were John Sewell of Leeds who was in the second-row and Brian Howard of St Helens who was Sully's centre partner. The pair worked well together as the RAF won 6–3 despite being penalised frequently.

He was again chosen, along with Howard and Sewell, against the Army at Twickenham on Saturday 26 March. While it was rare against the Navy, finding a familiar professional face or two amongst the opposition was fairly regular when playing against the Army. For this match, Sully and Brian Howard found themselves facing up to an Army centre partnership of Phil Jackson (Royal Signals and Barrow) and Sid Lowdon (Royal Artillery and Whitehaven). There was an even greater familiarity with another Army player; Brian Gabbitas (Royal Signals and Hunslet) was their stand-off.

A draw was all that was required for the RAF to become champions. That did not look likely when the Army held a 6–0 lead well into the second half. With time running out, Sully combined with his stand-off, Mel Channer, to score a try. Later, Channer kicked a penalty to level the scores, 6–6, and that was enough to make the RAF the champions.

RAF commitments meant that Sully did not play for Huddersfield again until Saturday 9 April when his basic training was complete. Even with leave approved, getting to matches was not always easy. Cars were not allowed on camp, but according to one of Sully's friends at West Kirby, Jack Musgrave, that did not stop him. He had a car, a maroon Wolsey 444, which he kept hidden away. Sully would loan it out to his comrades, but never disclose its hideaway.

Sully's good humour made him a popular addition to the RAF squad. The RAF had a strong fixture schedule playing the major English clubs, such as Bedford, Coventry, Harlequins, Gloucester, Leicester and Wasps, Oxford and Cambridge Universities, leading Welsh clubs such as

Swansea as well as representative teams including the British Police and Civil Service.

John Mace relates a tale that travelling back from a win at Swansea, the RAF Rugby Union's treasurer, an Air Commodore no less, told Sully he was pleased that he seemed to be enjoying playing rugby union. Apparently Sully confirmed this, but not quite in the way the senior officer probably hoped for: "Ee I do that. Have you ever sat in a rugby league coach having cost each of the team a £15 bonus, by dropping a scoring pass?"

It was not just rugby union that was on offer in the armed forces at this time. A couple of weeks after appearing at Twickenham, Sully turned out for the British Services Rugby League team against the French Services. Played at Headingley on the afternoon of Wednesday 13 April, the British team won 15–7. Although he did not get on the scoresheet, Sully's powerful running in the centre was noted. This was a match organised by the RFL, who had a wealth of talent doing national service to choose from at the time. A couple of matches were played, but then the fixture was dropped.

Sully ended the season with Huddersfield at Workington. The visitors lost 33–8, but Lionel Cooper, making his last appearance for the club, managed to score a try, his 65th of the season for Huddersfield. Cooper was then free to concentrate on his benefit events that were lined up over the summer. Part of his benefit was a brochure produced by the Huddersfield Supporters' Club. In it, Cooper picked the All-Star team in which he would have liked to have played and named young Sully as his reserve back. He went on to praise his young centre saying "I mention Mick Sullivan as a reserve because in my eight years in English football I feel he is the best prospect I have seen. Speed, brains, courage, determination and, above all, a willingness to learn, in fact all the essentials of a great player."

Once again success had eluded Huddersfield; knocked out of the Yorkshire Cup in the second round and the Challenge Cup in the first round. In the NRL, Huddersfield had scored more tries and more points than any other club, but could only finish 11th in the table, well away from a place in the Championship play-offs. Despite his international and RAF commitments, by the end of the season Sully had scored 14 tries in 29 league and cup matches for Huddersfield.

Playing for Huddersfield.
(Courtesy Robert Gate)

5. League and union

The close season prior to the start of the 1955–56 campaign saw another major member of Huddersfield's Wembley team depart. Despite many attempts to get him to change his mind, Lionel Cooper had confirmed his decision to retire. It looked like being a season very similar to the previous one, no new recruits of any standing having been brought to the club. Some talented youngsters such as Frank Dyson were coming through the ranks and others such as Austin Kilroy from Batley and Tommy Smales from Featherstone Rovers were being recruited, but they were all ones for the future. Sully could look forward to taking over the left-wing position, but that was to be shared with Cooper's compatriot, Johnny Hunter, who was no longer an automatic choice at full-back.

Having already made a good impression at international level in the World Cup, Sully seemed this season to be climbing the representative ladder, but in reverse order. The first step down was to make his England debut. After a year's break for the inaugural World Cup tournament, the International Championship resumed this season. With Wales merged into the Other Nationalities team, England played just two matches. The terms offered to the English team were £10 for a win, £7 for a draw and £6 for a defeat. Travelling expenses were paid based on third-class rail fares.

The opening match against Other Nationalities at Wigan's Central Park was scheduled very early, on the evening of Monday 12 September. The English team was outplayed and outscored, seven tries to two, by a combination of six Welshmen, three Australians, two Irishmen, one New Zealander and a Scot. Sully enhanced his growing reputation by making the most of a thin try-scoring chance on the right wing. England lost 33–16.

Four days after playing for Huddersfield at Leigh, Sully made his Yorkshire debut on the left wing against the touring New Zealanders on Wednesday 21 September at Hull KR's Craven Park. The Kiwis had arrived carrying injuries and were struggling on the field. They had drawn their first match and narrowly lost the next two matches. Sully's County debut, which brought him an extra £50 from Huddersfield, looked like being an easy victory and he scored two tries, but the Kiwis defied the odds to register a surprise 33–17 win.

Having played against Featherstone Rovers at Fartown on the Saturday, Sully appeared in the centre for Yorkshire against Lancashire at Oldham's Watersheddings ground on Monday 26 September. Lancashire dominated the first half and although the white rose responded after the break, the home side won comfortably 26–10.

Two days later, Sully was appearing on the newly launched commercial television channel. The RFL had approved a tournament promoted by Associated Rediffusion, the company which was running the London Independent Television franchise, and Huddersfield was one of eight clubs that picked up £400 to enter. Their first round match, against Wigan at Woolwich Stadium, was played on the evening of Wednesday 28 September. Unfortunately, only London viewers were able to watch Sully contribute a try as Huddersfield got the better of Wigan 33–11. Sadly, only the two clubs with the best winning margins would proceed to the final and Huddersfield missed out by two points.

Because Yorkshire's second match against Cumberland was scheduled just three days before the first test against the Kiwis, Sully was one of six players (the others being Gordon Brown, Jeff Stevenson, Jack Wilkinson, Basil Watts and Don Robinson) who could not be considered for selection. Despite having to field a depleted team, Yorkshire won at Bradford to finish as runners-up in the three team County Championship.

Sully was one of only three of Great Britain's World Cup winners to retain his place for the first test which was held at Swinton on Saturday 8 October. The rest of the team was made up of six from the last unsuccessful Ashes campaign down under and four new caps. To try and ensure that this untried combination did not suffer any unnecessary mishaps, the selectors said that the players would assemble for special training at Blackpool on Wednesday 5 October.

As a newcomer, Sully would not have known all of his teammates too well, but there was one familiar face at Blackpool. On the personal initiative of the stand-in team manager, James Hilton, Joe Egan, Hilton's club coach, was on hand to assist Alan Prescott, the new skipper, prepare the team, but only in an honorary capacity. In the time available, the pair laid particular emphasis on developing an understanding among the forwards.

In those days, New Zealand tour parties lacked the top-flight experience necessary to mount a serious challenge to a British test team. Home crowds expected to be entertained by the Kiwis' open style of play, but did not really expect them to be able to win against hardened British combinations.

Sully's first test on home soil did not get off to a good start because an injury to Don Robinson reduced Great Britain to 12 men after only nine minutes. Great Britain put in a dogged performance and thanks to two tries from Sully reached the interval 8–3 ahead. After the break, he had a third try disallowed for a forward pass. Things got even tougher when Billy Boston had to go off the field for 10 minutes which reduced the British side to just 11 men. Undaunted, the depleted British team rallied and set up three tries in the last 12 minutes to inflict a humiliating 25–16 defeat on the Kiwis.

There was a gap of over five weeks between the first two tests, but Sully did not lose contact with the Kiwis. Four earlier defeats against club teams offered the possibility of a home win when the Kiwis arrived at Fartown on Saturday 22 October, but Huddersfield could never get on top and lost 25–16.

Having been thought to lack cohesion at times, the British team was brought together at Leeds on Thursday 10 November and special coaching sessions, focusing on developing understanding and planned moves, were held later that day and on Friday at Castleford.

1955 Great Britain test team.
(Photo: Courtesy *Rugby League Journal*)

The following day at Odsal Stadium, it was time for the players to show what they had learned at those sessions. Sully had obviously learnt a lot. A superb individual burst brought him his first try. His second was scored in the corner after a Stevenson break and the last, for his hat-trick, through a great diagonal run to the opposite corner with just over 10 minutes remaining made the game safe. As the Lions relaxed, the Kiwis responded with two late tries. They could not save the series, but did make the result a more respectable 27–12 defeat.

In what was a very crowded international calendar, space was found for two 'unofficial' test matches against France. These matches were the last two of five meetings between the two countries in the early 1950s that were not granted full test status.

The first was at the Parc des Princes in Paris on Sunday 11 December 1955. Starved of possession, Sully was virtually unemployed until the last minute, when he ran inside to take a reverse pass from his centre Alan Davies to score an unconverted try. Lewis Jones succeeded with the conversion to complete Great Britain's scoring in a 17–5 defeat. However, there was some good news – a late night party was laid on for the team at the Moulin Rouge.

Fielding a virtually unchanged team, only Terry Hollindrake had not played in Paris, Great Britain's management was so confident going into the final test against New Zealand, which was held six days later, that no training session was organised beforehand. After all, no British team had ever lost a test match at Headingley and the Kiwis were weakened by injuries. The British took the field confident that a clean sweep was on the cards, but it did not turn out that way. The Kiwis were always in control, but Sully grabbed a try on 75 minutes, which Lewis Jones converted, to make the final score, a 28–13 defeat, slightly more respectable. When the Kiwis departed for France they must have been glad to see the back of Sully because he had run in 10 tries in his five appearances against them.

Away from the international arena, a bad run of injuries had undermined Huddersfield's challenge for honours. A disastrous Christmas programme that saw a defeat at Bramley on Christmas Eve, a home defeat by Halifax on Boxing Day and a 34–0 hammering at Thrum Hall the following day left the Fartowners down in 23rd place with just seven wins from 20 matches.

From such a lowly position, the only way was up. A run of victories in the New Year lifted the spirits of the club and supporters, but the consistency necessary to really move up the table was lacking. Victories over Whitehaven and Swinton in the first two rounds of the Challenge Cup, in which Sully crossed for three tries seemed to indicate that there might be good things to come. However, in the third round, with Sully absent on RAF duty at Twickenham, Wigan proved far too good at Central Park and won 24–2.

Union with the RAF

Aircraftman Sullivan was now conveniently stationed at RAF Yeadon near Leeds. After Christmas, Sully was required by the RAF Union's team managers and with his rugby league representative matches as well he missed many of Huddersfield's matches. It was a major challenge, but the RAF XV did well recording 11 wins in as many matches in the run up to Inter-service tournament.

Just before the tournament's customary opening match, RAF versus the Navy, on Saturday 16 February, severe winter weather set in. The RAF's match at Leicester on Thursday 2 February had to be cancelled and the match against the Navy was postponed.

Huddersfield's relationship with the RAF Rugby Union remained good and the latter agreed that Sully could step down from their team to play Bedford on 3 March and instead play at Swinton in the Challenge Cup. Two weeks before the meeting with the Army, the young airmen inflicted a particularly severe defeat on Gloucester, winning 22–3 on Saturday 10 March. After the match, Tom Voyce, the legendary former Gloucester and England rugby union flanker, commented that Sully was the finest wing threequarter ever seen at Kingsholm.

He was selected on the right wing, with Brian Howard as his centre, against the Army on Saturday 24 March. Huddersfield again requested his services, but there was no chance of them succeeding. Sully was needed at Twickenham where he found himself in direct opposition to Ike Southward (Royal Artillery and Workington Town). The RAF got the better of an Army XV reduced to 14 men in the second half to record a comfortable 26–9 victory. Sully's performance on attack and defence was complimented; particularly his ability to create tries for others.

Sully and Brian Howard kept their places as the right wing pairing for the rearranged match against the Royal Navy at Twickenham on Saturday 2 April, which the airmen lost 11–9. With each service having won one match, the tournament ended in a three-way tie.

Sully's season continued with a couple of international league matches. The first was the second unofficial test against France, which was held under lights at Odsal Stadium on Wednesday 11 April. A close contest swung Britain's way after a French forward, Berthomieu, was sent off with a quarter of an hour still to play. Sully had a good game and scored one of Great Britain's four tries in an 18–10 win.

Four days later, he appeared once more on the left wing for the English Services' Rugby League team. This proved to be the last meeting of the two nations at this level. Once again the party travelled by air from Blackbushe for the match in Marseilles. A well prepared French Services' team were allowed to build up a 15–0 first half lead and a second half fightback by the English Services was unable to close such a substantial gap. The match ended with the French 18–10 ahead.

Freed from his RAF commitments, Sully returned to the Huddersfield side for the start of the club's Easter programme. He played against Hull KR on Saturday 20 April alongside a Welsh debutant – Ray Cecil – who occupied the left centre berth. Sully scored a try but the match finished as a 16–14 defeat at Craven Park.

Everyone associated with the club knew new blood was desperately needed at Fartown. Any hopes of new experienced Australian talent arriving at Fartown had been dashed when the international transfer ban had been extended in the summer of 1955. The lack of recruits from the southern hemisphere was exacerbated by a lack of interest in the Scottish borders and by what Welsh talent there was available becoming a more risky investment and less affordable. Not that the club had not tried to bring players from south Wales, a region from which it had made few direct signings since the war.

According to press reports, Cliff Morgan, the Wales and British Lions stand-off who had just returned from touring South Africa, rejected an offer of £5,000 from Huddersfield, plus an additional £2,000 from a Sunday newspaper, in November 1955. Huddersfield's scouts had to keep searching and they finally secured the signature of Ray Cecil, a stand-off or centre from Newport. There must have been many envious eyes in the dressing room when newspaper reports gave the player, who had not won international honours, a signing on fee as £3,000, far higher than most of them would have hoped to receive.

There was just time for a couple more appearances, which brought three tries, before the domestic season closed in mid-April. Having started early in the season, the International Championship did not conclude until its final days. Even that was in doubt for a while as the RFL and FRL struggled to agree on an acceptable date for the final match. Despite it clashing with the Championship final, England took on France at Lyon on Thursday 10 May. Sully retained his place on the right wing. Although he had not played for three weeks, he scored one of England's three tries in a 23–9 defeat. Having suffered a second defeat, England finished bottom of the International Championship table. Other Nationalities were crowned the champions with two victories.

It was a poignant outcome. A lack of qualified new blood, due to a combination of the international signing ban and a slowdown in the recruitment of Welsh players, led to the decision to disband the Other Nationalities team at the end of the season and suspend the International Championship. The England team was put into hibernation for the next six years.

Scoring for Huddersfield.

The season had not gone entirely to plan for Sully. Johnny Hunter's presence had not allowed him to completely take over Lionel Cooper's old position. As a result it meant that Sully's 30 appearances in the first team, two of them friendlies, had been split, 18 on the wing and 12 in the centre. On the positive side there had been more victories than defeats, but fourteenth in the NRL was hardly satisfactory especially as the club went out early in both knockout cups. When looking back in the *1956 Fartown Rugby League Year Book*, Hubert Lockwood, the chairman of the Football Committee, could only describe 1955–56 as "a disappointing season from a playing and financial point of view".

While disappointing for the club, on a personal level it had been a good season for Sully. Despite some bad luck with injuries, especially in October and November, which adversely affected the team's performance, Sully had still managed to record 25 tries in his 28 appearances for Huddersfield to add to the 13 tries he scored in 10 representative matches. A total of 38 tries put him seventh in the try-scoring list. The *Fartown Rugby League Yearbook* said that Sully had missed many games through international or RAF matches, but had "showed his usual strong running and averaged practically a try a game". He had scored two hat-tricks, against Keighley and Hull KR.

6. For club and country

For the forthcoming 1956–57 campaign, the NRL programme had been increased from 36 to 38 matches. As usual the League's members were divided into Lancashire and Yorkshire county groups with 15 clubs in each. The county provided each of its clubs with 28 fixtures to which were then added another 10 against five members of the other county. For a club like Huddersfield, it represented a fixture formula that reduced travelling over to Lancashire to a minimum outside the Challenge Cup and the Championship play-offs.

The season kicked off with the usual friendly against Halifax on Monday 13 August. Sully ran in two tries at Fartown in the opening League match against Castleford five days later. After missing the next two matches he returned to claim a hat-trick at Fartown in a victory over Bradford Northern on Wednesday 29 August.

Having travelled to Barrow with Huddersfield on the Saturday for a 24–15 defeat, Sully returned to the north-west with Yorkshire to play against Cumberland at The Recreation Ground, Whitehaven on Wednesday 19 September. A makeshift Cumbrian team achieved an unexpected last minute victory 15–14. Some Yorkshire committee members tried to pin the blame on the long coach journey to Whitehaven that their team had made on the morning of the match.

That explanation did not prevent the county selectors making wholesale changes ahead of the match against Lancashire one week later. Only Featherstone's Don Fox retained his position in the back division. For some reason the selectors decided to swap around their left wing pairing, so Sully moved to left centre while his partner, Wakefield's Don Froggett took over on the wing. Whether the switch would have worked was never tested because before the match Sully was refused leave by the RAF and had to withdraw.

Sully's form remained good and he appeared in the Great Britain team in a test trial against the Rest of the League at Odsal Stadium on Wednesday 3 October, and scored a try in a 26–23 win. At full-back for Great Britain was Frank Dyson, who like Sully had progressed through the ranks at Fartown and was now on the verge of the sport's highest honours.

Sully was one of nine members of the Great Britain XIII who were selected for the first test, but his team mate Frank Dyson missed out for now. In reality, there never appeared to be an obvious alternative on the field, as Sully's opposite number in the trial, his club mate, the former All Black, Peter Henderson, was one of three members of the Rest who were not eligible for British selection.

There was an extra international match this season. In what appears to have been a warm up before the Australians arrived, a NRL XIII met France at Marseilles on Sunday 21 October. The RFL's intentions were somewhat undermined when the county cup finals were scheduled for the previous day. None of the players who would be taking part in those matches were considered which meant four changes (Frank Mortimer, Alan Davies, Alan Prescott, Brian Shaw) to the probable test team. Sully was not affected and scored a try in the 18–17 win.

Even though the Armed Forces were on high alert because of the Suez crisis, Sully remained available for Huddersfield and scored tries in the victories over Featherstone Rovers at Fartown and at the Barley Mow over Bramley on the following Saturday.

This season the four-year tour cycle that the sport followed brought a visit from the Kangaroos. There would be a slight difference this time. The decision that the Australian party would not leave for Europe until after their own domestic season ended meant that this season's tour started later and the itinerary had to be shortened. Three of the usual fixtures cut from the tour's itinerary were those against the county teams.

As a result, Sully's first encounter with the Kangaroos was with Huddersfield at Fartown on Saturday 10 November, one week before the first test. Although a new look Kangaroo squad had lost to four club teams by then, Huddersfield struggled against a near test strength Australian side. It was a poignant match with Johnny Hunter taking on his fellow countrymen in Huddersfield's colours for the last time. Sentiment, however, was not enough for the home team. Although Sully scored a try, Huddersfield lost 20–10.

He kept his place in the test team; the terms for the British players were reported as £14 for a win and £8 for a defeat. Money was not the only thing on Sully's mind. While staying in Blackpool ahead of the first Test, he received a telegram on Friday 16 November telling him that

Jean, after a difficult pregnancy, had given birth to their first child, David, at Moorlands Maternity Home in Dewsbury.

The following day the new dad played well on another muddy pitch, made a try with a short kick through for Jack Grundy in the first half and scored one himself later in the second half as the Lions drew first blood with a 21–10 win over Australia at Wigan.

Two weeks later, a much changed Australian team caused Great Britain major problems at a muddy Odsal. Back play was kept to a minimum, as two evenly matched packs slogged it out. The scores were level 7–7 at half-time, but in the last quarter the Australians took control and ran in four tries to win 22–9.

The deciding test was two weeks later at Swinton's Station Road. Phil Jackson was concussed early in the match and Sully took over his centre spot. Sully finished off a 40 yard passing movement to score a try halfway through the second half. In winning 19–0, Great Britain had the satisfaction of 'nilling' the Kangaroos to regain the Ashes.

The first official Test match between Great Britain against France was played on Saturday 26 January 1957 at Headingley. From the kick-off, the British team dominated and Sully scored a try halfway through the first half. Although Great Britain led 19–2 at half-time, France closed the margin early in the second half before the home team regained the initiative to seal a 45–12 win.

The second Test against France was played at Toulouse on Sunday 3 March. It turned into a roughhouse match as the French desperately tried to get the series back on level terms. Despite an adverse penalty count, the British team held the lead with 10 minutes to go before an overly partisan local referee allowed France to equalise and the match finished as a draw, 19–19.

Sully played in an unchanged Great Britain team against France at Knowsley Road, St Helens on Wednesday 10 April. He had little to do on the left wing in the first half, but after the break swapped places with the injured Phil Jackson. Within two minutes, playing right centre, He had straightened out of a move and a burst of speed enabled him to score his first try. Ten minutes later, he made a try for Lewis Jones before signing off, with just a minute left, with a solo try. Between those two scores, two French tries made the final score 29–14, to make the British victory look less emphatic than it had been.

41

1957 Great Britain team that played France at St Helens in April 1957.
Great Britain won 29–14; Sully scored two tries.
(Photo: Courtesy *Rugby League Journal*)

Promotion in the RAF

In spite of being excused so many military duties, Sully had been promoted to senior aircraftman, but it was still his services on the rugby pitch that were most in demand. There was still plenty of give-and-take between Huddersfield and the RAF RU, but sometimes no compromise was possible. Huddersfield wanted to play him in the Challenge Cup first round at Swinton, but the RAF's selectors were adamant he would be playing for them on what would be the last day of his National Service. The airmen won out and Sully appeared on the right wing against the Royal Navy for his fifth and final appearance at Twickenham on Saturday 9 February 1957. After leading 3–0 at half-time, the RAF surrendered the initiative and eventually lost 8–6. Defeat was a sad way to bring down the curtain on Sully's time in the RAF.

Sully had been asked to stay on for the second match against the Army, six weeks later, but was adamant he was going back to civilian life. All there was left to do was to collect his Certificate of Service and bring his National Service to a close. Then it was time for Sully to get on with the things he wanted to do.

While the RAF was losing to the Navy, 200 miles to the north, in Manchester, Huddersfield had been held to a 5–5 draw. There was no question now over his availability and Sully was back on the left wing for the replay, held the following Wednesday, when he scored a try in a 5–0 victory at Fartown.

When he returned to Fartown as a civilian, Sully found that Alec Fiddes had been brought back to the club as coach in January. Hopes of a good run in the Challenge Cup grew after Huddersfield had beaten Salford 6–2 at the Willows on Saturday 23 February. Those hopes proved short-lived because two weeks later, the eventual finalists, Barrow, won easily 10–0 in the third round. That defeat ended any hopes of honours finding their way to Fartown that season. Sully's final act was to score two tries as Huddersfield's League season ended with a defeat, 20–14, at Belle Vue on Saturday 27 April.

Once again it had been a relatively disappointing campaign. Huddersfield had started well and been in the top four at the end of October but had fallen away later and finished ninth in the NRL. They had been knocked out of Yorkshire Cup in the second round and out of the Challenge Cup in the third. With so many demands on his time, Sully had missed 13 matches, but had scored 26 tries in his 32 appearances for Huddersfield. But, in his 26 League appearances, Huddersfield had won only 13 times, which meant Sully had picked up losing money for half his work.

As required by law, Sully's job had been kept open during National Service so he was able to take up where he had left off as a plumber. His apprenticeship over, he would have been looking forward to earning some good money as a qualified plumber. For a full week he would have been looking forward to the day when he might collect £10, but the game's demands on his time would eat into that figure on a regular basis.

At a time of rising expectations, the game and the day job together should have provided a comfortable if not well paid life. Sully's prospects suffered an immediate setback when his employer in Pudsey decided that as the game was placing ever greater demands on his time they would have to let him go. Needing new employment, Mick and Jean decided to sell up in Dewsbury and buy a fish and chip shop in Pudsey.

Left: Mick and David.

Middle: Mick with the family car.

Bottom: Mick, Jean and David at home.

7. The 1957 World Cup

After the success of the inaugural World Cup competition, a second tournament was organised to celebrate the golden jubilee of the sport in Australia. Rather than having to wait to the customary Lions tour which came around every fourth summer, Sully had the opportunity to go to the southern hemisphere in summer 1957.

The World Cup party of 18 was announced on 1 April to give the players the chance to arrange time off work with their employers. Not surprisingly the selectors had based the tour party around that season's successful Test team. Only Austin Rhodes, a Great Britain reserve against France, was not already an international. However, Huddersfield's only representative in the party was Sully. Once the league programme was over there were a few evening training sessions, at Parkside, Watersheddings and Central Park, but Sully had to take a lot of the responsibility for keeping himself fit for five weeks.

While the party waited to depart the RL Council deliberated on what the players' payments would be. It was decided that that the players would receive £100 for the short tour in instalments, but some Council members argued this was too low. To pacify the dissenters it was agreed to review the payment when the party returned home.

A young, but not inexperienced party left Leeds for London on Saturday 1 June and arrived after stops in Rome, Karachi, Calcutta and Singapore in Perth on 4 June. Led by Alan Prescott as captain-coach, Great Britain, the holders, with series victories over New Zealand, Australia and France to their credit, travelled as favourites for the tournament. The party faced an itinerary of nine matches plus a couple of additional 'special' fixtures.

No British party had ever made a short visit to Australasia and the team managers seemed unsure of how to deal with its challenges. On this trip, there was no time available for the usual gradual build up to recover match fitness. All that had been arranged was for the party to undergo some preliminary training with the Western Australia Aussie Rules team and then play a warm-up match in Perth. Sully played against a weak Western Australia team at Perth on Sunday 9 June, and scored seven tries in a 66–5 win. That easy win proved costly for the Lions. Their stand-off, Warrington's Ray Price, suffered an ankle injury, which ruled him out of action for the rest of the trip.

45

The Lions then flew on to Sydney where they settled into the Pacific View Hotel at Manly. The holders' World Cup campaign would begin with a re-run of their last match, three years earlier, against France, this time at the SCG on Saturday 15 June. On a rain-soaked pitch the Lions proved the better of two teams, both of which were suffering from a longish lay-off. Sully scored the first British try, converted by Lewis Jones, who shortly afterwards was flattened and suffered a badly cut mouth. When Jones moved out to the wing, Sully switched to stand-off. After the break, Jones resumed at stand-off before Sully scored his second and Great Britain's last try in a 23–15 opening win.

There was just a two day turn around because the meeting of Great Britain and Australia was scheduled for the Monday of the Queen's Birthday holiday weekend, again at the SCG. Victory over the French had come at a price. Phil Jackson and Geoff Gunney had picked up injuries and two test debutants – Eric Ashton and Johnny Whiteley – had to be brought in. Disruption to the first choice team was compounded by a risky selection which saw the Lions take the field with five players carrying injuries.

Just when they needed some good fortune, bad luck struck. Alan Davies, the Lions' centre, suffered a serious thigh injury which caused him to leave the field. Great Britain, then trailing 5–4, had to play for the remaining hour with only 12 men. Hull's Johnny Whiteley moved to take over from Davies in the threequarters, but the Lions' five-man pack could not hold the Australians' six and Britain heavily, 31–6.

The 1957 Great Britain World Cup squad. Back: Harris, Sullivan, Davies, Moses, Rhodes, Price; middle: Turner, Little, Grundy, Gunney, Ashton, Whiteley, Boston; front: McKinney, Jackson, Fallowfield (manager), Prescott, Rawson (manager), Stevenson, Jones. (Photo: Courtesy Robert Gate)

Once Australia had beaten France three days earlier, Great Britain's meeting with New Zealand at the SCG on Tuesday 25 June was effectively to determine which country finished as runner-up. Only 11 of the British party were fit enough to train on the Saturday. One of those temporarily out of action was Sully with a leg muscle injury, but he was expected to be passed fit.

He was, and scored the Lions' second try which put them into the lead 10–2, but by half-time they were trailing 15–13. An injury hit Great Britain played poorly, but almost stole victory when a late Eric Ashton touchdown was ruled out. A 29–21 defeat meant the Lions, thanks to a marginally superior points' difference, finished a poor second to Australia in the competition table.

Sully was overlooked for the Rest of the World XIII that lost to the champions, Australia, at the SCG on Saturday 29 June. With the World Cup competition completed the British team embarked on a short series of matches that keep them in shape until it was time for a series of exhibition matches to start in South Africa.

The first match, against Queensland, was held at Brisbane's Lang Park, the recently opened home of the Queensland Rugby League on Monday 1 July. Sully scored three tries in a 44–5 win. In those pre-State of Origin days, the Maroons were restricted to those playing in the state, but this was still a superb British performance in very wet conditions against a Queensland team that contained six current Australian internationals.

With a victory in Brisbane behind them, the tourists flew off to New Zealand. Sully played against a French XIII in Auckland on Saturday 6 July. The Lions overturned a 12–3 half-time deficit to win 26–12.

Sully was one of seven Britons chosen for the Northern Hemisphere XIII that met New Zealand at Carlaw Park, Auckland two days later. Although something of an exhibition, this match was granted test status by the New Zealand Rugby League. In the first half the home side did not play like it was a test and went in at the break 19–2 down. Injuries to two of the French contingent – Levy and Appelian – reduced the Northern Hemisphere team to 11 men in the second half, but they hung on to beat a 12-man New Zealand 34–31. Sully scored a try.

That match concluded the team's time in the Antipodes. Controversially, the RFL and the French Rugby League had agreed with a local businessman, Ludwig Japhet, to return home via South Africa where three exhibition matches would be played to introduce the game to the local sporting public. In those pre-television days, playing in the country was the only way to give South African sports fans first-hand knowledge of rugby league. For this extra leg of the tour the players received £20 each from the South African promoters.

After a long journey from Auckland via Sydney and Mauritius, the Lions arrived in Johannesburg with only 15 players – Billy Boston and Alan Davies having already been sent home. Boston's injury saved the British management a major problem as Bill Boston would not have been welcome under apartheid in South Africa. In addition Phil Jackson and Ray Price were carrying injuries that would rule them out of playing for the rest of the trip.

Unfortunately, the matches were marked by a serious lack of interest and commitment on the part of both the British and French teams. There was also a marked degree of ill feeling that led to a number of violent incidents.

There were a few days to acclimatise to the altitude before the first match on Saturday 20 July. The venue was in Benoni, a gold mining city a few miles east of Johannesburg, which was 5,397 feet (1,645 m) above sea level. In the tough conditions, defence appeared to be optional. Sully scored a hat-trick as the Lions won 61–41.

After that encounter, it was down to sea-level for the next two matches. Bill Fallowfield, the RFL secretary, and one of the tour managers, later recalled how he had "read the 'riot act' to our players and they really did try for the second game. Unfortunately the same could not be said of the French team and we ran out easy winners." On 24 July, Sully scored twice, as the Lions won comfortably, 32–11.

Unfortunately for the spectators, play in the third match, at East London three days later, reverted to that seen in the first. Sully bagged one of the Lions' 15 tries in what was an embarrassingly easy victory; the Lions winning 69–11. Overall the South African spectators had been treated to a poor exhibition of what rugby league had to offer.

Once the final whistle had blown in East London, it was time to head back to Johannesburg and catch the flight to Manchester and home on Wednesday 31 July. Sully had made 10 appearances on tour, scoring 20 tries (60 points). There was some further good news in September; the RL Council had reviewed the World Cup payments and agreed that each player should receive a bonus of £50.

8. Moving on

Sully arrived home just as Huddersfield's pre-season training for the 1957–58 campaign was about to begin. Before he had left for Australia, he knew that Huddersfield's team would have to cope without several significant players who had retired – Jim Bowden, Bill Griffin and Johnny Hunter. By the time he was back in training at Fartown, it was clear that once again there was no significant new blood coming in.

Within a couple of weeks of being home the new season was underway. But before it did there was an incident that soured his relationship with the club. Sully had not claimed any pre-season training expenses and put in one composite claim as the season was about to begin. When Arthur Archbell's assistant saw it – for £17/10 (£17.50) – he refused to pay until he had checked with higher authority. That refusal marked a turning point and Norman Wainwright remembers that as he was given a lift back to Bradford Sully's mind was clearly made up; he would be looking for pastures new. This was not good news for Huddersfield's directors, who were only too aware that the club's only other experienced winger, Peter Henderson, would be making his way home to New Zealand in September.

Sully was obviously in fine form. He scored a hat-trick in front of his home crowd in the opening friendly against Halifax on Saturday 10 August. He held his form when the competitive matches got underway and did even better against Batley; he scored six tries in the first round Yorkshire Cup tie on Saturday 31 August.

Once again a trip to Barrow, where he scored a try, preceded a recall by the Yorkshire selectors. To accommodate Oldham's John Etty, who was recalled after a gap of eight years, Sully was selected as left centre, in a much changed Yorkshire team that took on Cumberland at the Boulevard, Hull on Wednesday 11 September. Sully scored a try and made one for his winger, Etty, in a 27–18 win.

Sully was back in Huddersfield's colours for a difficult visit to Wakefield on Monday 16 September. In atrocious weather the visitors just edged home 13–10 to book a place in the Yorkshire Cup semi-final and send Peter Henderson home to New Zealand on a high note.

Sully had scored four tries against Castleford at Fartown on the Saturday and maintained his scoring rate as a centre once more for

Yorkshire against Lancashire at Widnes's Naughton Park on Monday 23 September. This time he scored two tries to help Yorkshire beat the defending champions 25–11. Two wins meant Yorkshire reclaimed the County Championship and brought Sully his first winner's medal.

At Headingley five days later, Huddersfield managed to withstand a spirited Leeds fightback before Sully scored a brilliant try to make the game safe at 14–2.

Having reached the Yorkshire Cup Final, Huddersfield had to postpone the league visit of Wigan to Fartown which had been set for that day, 19 October. Instead, Huddersfield travelled over to Headingley again, this time to meet York. Huddersfield's team that day was: Frank Dyson, Harry Plunkett, Austin Kilroy, Roland Barrow, Mick Sullivan, Peter Ramsden, Tommy Smales, Ted Slevin, Roy Wood, David Flint, Brian Briggs, Ken Bowman, Dave Valentine (capt).

Although he was carrying an injury for most of the match, Huddersfield won 15–8 to bring Sully his first, and as it turned out, only senior honour with the club.

After four barren seasons some silverware had at last returned to Fartown, but not everyone associated with the club was happy. The Final turned out to be Sully's last appearance for Huddersfield. Unable to get him to change his mind, four days after the final, Huddersfield 's board reluctantly placed him on the transfer list, without bothering to tell him, at a prohibitive fee that was nearly twice the then record.

Even at such a fee a number of clubs were said to be interested. Leeds, Oldham, St Helens and Workington Town were among those mentioned, but Wigan's board – having been tipped off by a press contact – were the most decisive. They immediately made an official approach to Huddersfield. Backed by a £5,000 donation from their Supporters' Club, two Wigan directors, Bill Gore and Tom Hesketh, and the club secretary, Jack Wood, travelled over to Pudsey, where Sully was already in bed by the time they arrived. He roused himself, made them a cup of tea, listened to Wigan's offer and signed in the early hours of 23 October. The Wigan delegation then set off to Huddersfield where they added Arthur Archbell's signature to complete the deal before morning broke.

As stipulated in his original contract, Sully received £500 from Huddersfield. Huddersfield received a fee of £9,500, nearly double the previous record, also set by Wigan when they had signed Harry Street from Dewsbury in August 1951. Sully told a reporter: "I don't think any rugby player is worth that. I told Wigan it was too much and intended to appeal but they would not listen. I have not got over the shock yet." Sully did quite quickly, especially as the size of the fee made him a celebrity for a time. The fee was a record until Oldham broke it by signing Ike Southward from Workington Town on 11 March 1959 for £10,650.

Sully had ended his Huddersfield career as an ever-present this season with 15 appearances and 19 tries. In total for Huddersfield, Sully had made 117 appearances, scoring 93 tries for 279 points.

When recollecting those times in an *Open Rugby* interview in 1982, Sully said "I know I won lots of international honours at Fartown, but I was scoring two and three times in a game and still drawing losing pay. I was staggered at the size of the fee, as I was unaware of what Huddersfield were asking. I felt no pressure at all in being a record transfer man; it was just nice to be, at last, in a team that won trophies."

Having just moved into a new home in Pudsey, the Sullivans were reluctant to up and leave immediately and it was agreed that for the rest of the season he would continue to train at Huddersfield and travel to Wigan one night per week. It was a generous arrangement because it was not common practice for outsiders to train at Fartown, but Sully at least had the company of Roy Booth, the former Yorkshire and current Worcestershire wicket-keeper who also had permission to use the facilities. Even making it once a week, the journey over to Wigan in those pre-motorway days was demanding, taking nearly five hours there and back. Once the season was over, Mick and Jean would have to decide when to take up Wigan's offer of a house.

Wigan

At a stroke the transfer record had risen alarmingly. Fees for the best players appeared to be spiralling beyond the means of most of the league's members and some saw the game's future being threatened by such financial madness. Commenting on it in the *Rugby League Gazette*, the editor, Norman Berry, said "You must remember that Wigan is the hub of the rugby league world. That is an undisputed fact and hardly needs stressing. They are about the only club that could raise such money ... and, at the same time, one of the few clubs that can recoup that money via the turnstile."

As Berry says there seems to have been no shortage of money at Central Park as the board was already in the late stages of negotiation to bring Fred Griffiths, a full-back, over from South Africa when Sully became available.

Wigan had been one of the main powerhouses of the game for the past 50 years and had enjoyed a period of great success in the late 1940s. However, Jim Sullivan's departure for St Helens in the summer of 1952 had proved to be a more of a disruption than expected. Sullivan's successors as coach, Maurice Hughes and Ted Ward, had been unable to get the team back on track for honours.

Signing for Wigan gave Sully the chance to team up once again with Joe Egan. After four years without any silverware making its way to Central Park, Joe Egan, a member of Sullivan's great post-war team, had been brought back to Wigan as manager-coach in August 1956. Egan arrived to find a team that had a lot of talented players, many of whom were local. Some shrewd acquisitions had enabled Egan to strengthen key positions from outside and by the start of his second season in charge the club appeared to be well on the road to recovery.

Sully had played test rugby with many of Wigan's big names – Billy Boston, Eric Ashton, Dave Bolton, John Barton and Brian McTigue – so there was not too much ice to break. Also on Wigan's books was Terry O'Grady, the 1954 British tourist, who had been brought from Oldham by Joe Egan at the start of the year to occupy the left wing position. All of a sudden Wigan had a surfeit of wing riches.

However, Sully's Wigan career did not get off to the best possible start when he travelled over for his first training session. It was an arduous journey at the best of times, but the terrible driving conditions encountered on the way that day meant he got lost over the Pennines and was 90 minutes late arriving at Central Park.

He made his Wigan debut, on the left-wing, against Leigh at Central Park on 26 October 1957 when the visitors won 9–7 in front of a 28,000 crowd. As expected, Sully's arrival although welcomed, gave the club's selection committee some problems. Initially, the selectors tried to accommodate Sully on the left wing by switching Terry O'Grady to the right and moving another test winger, Billy Boston, into the centre.

Making hay with Billy Boston at Wigan.

Further permutations included using Billy Boston at stand-off and Sully was also played at left centre. Such switches were acceptable enough to begin with, but a more settled line up was needed if success was to come to Central Park.

Sully's move to Wigan did not affect his test career. He kept his place for the opening match against France at Toulouse on Sunday 3 November 1957. Stricken with a dose of influenza on the day, he still managed to score a try in each half to help ensure a British win 25–15. Immediately after the match he went to bed with a sore throat and a temperature instead of going to the civic reception.

His second appearance for Great Britain against France this season was at his new home ground, Central Park, Wigan on Saturday 23 November 1957. While his club mates were losing on the other side of the Pennines at Hunslet, Sully managed to score a late try, one of three British tries in the last 14 minutes, in an emphatic 44–15 win.

Only a few weeks after arriving in the town, Oldham visited Central Park on 1 February. It turned into a brawling affair which the home side lost 9–6. In its report on the match, the *Wigan Examiner* obviously had its ideas on who instigated the brawling and warned that "Sullivan's hard, head-high tackling leads to losing of tempers and makes him a marked man for retaliation."

The Challenge Cup got underway on 8 February. Sully scored a hat-trick at Central Park to knock out a hapless Whitehaven 39–10. Both the next two rounds were away and Sully did not get on the score-sheet in either, although both ended in victory – at Wakefield, 11–5 on 22 February – and at Oldham, 8–0 a fortnight later.

With the key matches in the Cup campaign looming, it was time for test duty once more. Having won the first two matches there was little for Great Britain to play for when the third test finally came around at Grenoble on Sunday 2 March. Although the tour party had yet to be named, Jim Brough had already been appointed as the Lions' first official coach and he was able to travel with a virtually unchanged British team and both tour managers to France. With just a minute to go before half-time, France lost the ball, Sully grabbed it and raced 75 yards to score. Bernard Ganley converted to give Great Britain a 10–7 lead at the interval. Great Britain went on to win 23–9 and complete a series whitewash.

The Challenge Cup semi-final was held at Swinton on 29 March and there a Sully try proved crucial as Wigan just edged a victory, 5–3, over Rochdale Hornets. A place at Wembley had been secured, but before that the league campaign had to be completed. Despite winning the last five matches, in which Sully scored eight tries, not enough ground could be made up and in the end Wigan just missed out on a top-four play-off place by two points. In one of those five matches, on 16 April, Sully returned to Fartown for the rearranged match with Huddersfield. As captain for the day he scored two tries in a comfortable 31–11 win.

The Challenge Cup Final was the first to be covered by BBC Television for six years. Eddie Waring and Bill Fallowfield were the commentary team as Wigan took on Workington Town at Wembley on Saturday 10 May. The live broadcast of the final was blamed by many for the relatively poor attendance; only 66,109 were present to enjoy what turned out to be a very open and exciting match.

On the day, two passages of play brought home to those watching in the stadium and to millions more at home the two sides of Sully's on-field character. The first was his over-aggressive defence. Shortly after Ike Southward had put Town into the lead, Sully's high tackle laid out Workington's stand-off, Harry Archer, 15 minutes into the first half. Unlike today, Sully's high tackle only resulted in a penalty. The other side, his class, was soon on show. Wigan quickly capitalised on their numerical advantage. Billy Boston started a move that flowed right across the backs before Sully finished it off by crossing in the corner. Jackie Cunliffe converted, to level the scores at 5–5.

Although a badly concussed Harry Archer returned to the field after 10 minutes treatment, he was not able to play a full role for the rest of the match. Archer's incapacity and further serious injuries disrupted the Cumbrians, but Wigan only just managed to beat them, 13–9. It was a win nevertheless and it brought Sully his first major medal.

Sully ended the season as the sport's top scorer with a total of 50 tries. That total included 19 tries in his 15 league and cup appearances for Huddersfield, 24 tries in his 29 league and cup appearances for Wigan along with three tries for Yorkshire and four for Great Britain.

It was a mark of Sully's qualities as a winger that behind him in the try-scoring list that season were: Ike Southward (Workington Town) with 47, Warrington's Brian Bevan on 46, Bradford Northern's Malcolm Davies on 45 and teammate Billy Boston with 43.

Scoring for Wigan at Wembley in 1958.
(Photo: Courtesy *Rugby League Journal*)

The Wigan team with the Challenge Cup after beating Workington Town 13–9.
(Photo: Courtesy Robert Gate)

9. The 1958 Lions tour

Having travelled down under for the World Cup, Sully was keen to return with the Lions in 1958. Being chosen for the test team that won at Grenoble meant he was not required to appear in either of the tour trials. As expected, Sully was included when the International Committee met and announced the tour party on Saturday 22 March. He was listed as being 5 feet 10 inches in height and weighing 11 stone 12 pounds.

It was to be a long tour. The tourists would be away for over 12 weeks. In that time Sully would receive a £20 one-off payment upon arrival in Australia and then £3 per week for the duration of the tour. Meanwhile Jean would receive £3 each week plus an extra 10/- (£0.50) each week for David.

Sully and his three Wigan teammates, Eric Ashton, Dave Bolton and Brian McTigue, stayed on in London after the Challenge Cup Final and set off with the majority of the party which left from Heathrow on Monday 12 May on a three day, fault interrupted journey to Sydney. The players involved in the Championship final between Hull FC and Workington Town flew out a week later.

Sully's high tackle in the Cup Final had left an impression not only on his fellow tourist, Harry Archer, who complained of a headache for months afterwards, but also on Tom Mitchell, a Workington Town director who was one of the managers of the upcoming Australasian tour. Tom Mitchell recalls in his memoirs how, after only the second match of the tour, sensational headlines about Sully's high crash tackling caused him concern. He arranged to have a chat. Mitchell recalled Sully's response: "Now then Tom, referees, touch judges and others says ah's doing it, tha says ah's doing it – can tha see me doing it?" In turn Mitchell recalls he said "No, Mick, but from now on its got to stop or I am going to be minus a winger. You won't finish the tour. Back home for you!" At that Sully "gave his 'usual' mischievous grin, got the message and embarked on a major legal contribution in the search for the Ashes."

As the advance party contained only two wingers – Sully and St Helens' Frank Carlton – they had to play in the first two matches. Under the direction of St Helens' Alan Prescott and Barrow's Phil

Jackson, the captain and vice-captain respectively, the tourists prepared for the opening match at Wollongong on Sunday 18 May. Whoever had drawn up the itinerary had certainly not intended that the Lions should have an easy start. Their first opponents were Southern Districts, who had beaten the Lions in 1946 and 1950 and drawn with them in 1954. The Lions passed the test well. Sully scored two tries in a 36–18 victory. It was then on to Orange for a midweek match against Western Districts where Sully scored a try in a 24–24 draw.

By the time the party returned to Sydney, the second group was just arriving. Jim Brough assumed the coaching duties for the first time as the whole party got together on Friday 23 May. However, the tour party was hardly at full strength in terms of wingers. Frank Carlton had suffered a broken nose at Orange and Workington's Bill Wookey had arrived carrying a leg injury that had caused him to miss the Championship final. It meant that Sully and Ike Southward were the only fit wingers.

Up next was a match against Newcastle on Saturday 24 May. After scrum-half Frank Pitchford received a knock he was moved out to the wing, Harry Archer took over scrum responsibilities and Sully filled in at stand-off. Sully scored a try as the tourists won 35–16. This was rated a satisfactory performance early in the tour on a hot sunny day. Four days later, he was back on the wing for the match against Northern NSW at Tamworth. He scored two tries as the tourists won 27–17.

The fifth match was against Sydney at the SCG three days later. Facing a strong Sydney XIII containing 10 internationals, the tourists won 20–15. Finally, after playing in the first five matches, Sully was rested. Bill Wookey played in midweek against Riverina at Leeton.

Sully was recalled for the match against NSW at the SCG on Saturday 7 June. There was a great deal of tension in the build up to this match as a result of the events four years earlier. When the two teams had met at the SCG in July 1954 the match had descended into an all-out brawl and the referee walked off, abandoning the match 16 minutes into the second half. No one wanted a repeat of that on this tour and the night before the match the referee visited the tourists' hotel to deliver a sharp warning about dirty play.

As usual, it was a hard match against the 'Blues' and it was not until just before half-time that Sully backed up an Alex Murphy blindside break to score a try which when converted by Eric Fraser put the Lions ahead 9–8 at the break. The match had passed reasonably peacefully so far, but then 10 minutes into the second half Vince Karalius was dismissed. In the next 10 minutes he was followed by two Australians, Rex Mossop and Greg Hawick. The match continued to deteriorate and the NSW left winger, Peter Dimond, dashed downfield and raised his boot knee high as Sully braced to tackle him. For that Dimond was also dismissed. Despite their depleted numbers, the 'Blues' still led but a second Sully try, once again converted by Eric Fraser, retook the lead 14–10. The Lions held on to win 19–10.

At a tour meeting the following Wednesday a number of complaints came to the surface. Some were directed at Swinton's Bennett Manson, the other tour manager, but Jim Brough was also in the firing line. Believing that the players were not fit enough, Manson had imposed a blanket 10.30pm curfew. This was so unpopular that it had to be altered. It was agreed that the curfew would operate for the week before a test match and for the two days before any other match.

Jim Brough held very futuristic views on a player's lifestyle. His players were athletes and in his eyes his involvement with them went beyond the boundaries of the training field. Being ahead of his time meant his views were often not appreciated. One of his concerns was to get the players to eat the right food and cut down on their alcohol consumption. Believing that the players were being given too much meat in one of the hotels, Brough instructed the kitchen staff to reduce the amount. The players held that the amount of meat was right, but that the portions of vegetables were too small. After a clear-the-air meeting, Brough and the players reached a compromise – the hotel reinstated the meat and put some extra spoonfuls of vegetables on the plate. When questioned later, Tom Mitchell remarked that he thought only two of the players – Brian McTigue and Mick Martyn – were not spending all their £3 weekly tour allowance on extra food.

To make matters worse, Brough's coaching and training methods, which were based around a disciplined schedule, were not appreciated by many of the senior players. Taken all together there is no doubt that Brough made himself unpopular with most of, if not all, the players at various times on tour.

The first test was played at the SCG on Saturday 14 June. As holders of the World Cup, the Australians went into the match in confident mood. They ended it in the same way, having beaten Great

Britain 25–8 in front of a huge crowd, reported as 67,637. It had been a hard match during which Sully was cautioned for rough play by referee D'Arcy Lawler. By his own high standards, Sully did not have a good match. He dropped four passes, although two of them were described as being very awkward.

The day after the Test match a shaken Lions party flew to Brisbane. The tour management called a meeting at midday on Monday to review the situation. At that meeting Brough told the players that he was disgusted with their recent tour performances, and he included the first test in that category. They were left in no doubt that they had six matches to put things right before the 'must win' second test.

A damaged thigh, sustained in the first test, ruled Sully out of the floodlit evening encounter with Brisbane at the Exhibition Ground on Monday 16 June. Suspension and mounting injuries were causing problems and the Lions had only 16 players available for the match against Queensland at the Exhibition Ground on Saturday 21 June. The team selected performed superbly, and scored eight tries in a 36–19 victory. Sully scored two of those tries, but stubbed a toe badly and the initial assessment was that he would probably miss at least the next two matches.

In fact, the injury ruled Sully out of the next four matches. It was not all bad news for him, because he got to travel with the party northwards, first to Rockhampton and then on to Townsville where he was able to take in the tropical sights without having to struggle on the field in over 90 degree heat. Without him, the Lions ran out very easy winners over Central Queensland at Rockhampton the following day, Wide Bay at Bundaberg on Wednesday 25 June, Far North Queensland at Cairns on Saturday 28 June and North Queensland at Townsville on the Sunday. Next day the tourists flew back to Brisbane.

As it made its way through Queensland, the party realised that the tour had reached a critical phase. According to Bennett Manson, in a report by Joe Humphreys of the *Daily Mirror*, Jim Brough had approached him on 24 June, 11 days before the second test with a proposition: "Give me 15 players; let me take them away; train them and coach them in my way, and I guarantee that I will win you the second test." Apparently, Brough did not believe that the players could achieve the required fitness and the necessary resolution in the middle of the city.

The 1958 Lions squad. Back: Bolton, Carlton, Southward, Sullivan, Wookey, Moses, Archer; Standing: Martyn, McTigue, K. Jackson, Karalius, Brough (coach), Challinor, Terry, Fraser, Davies; Seated: Goodwin, Edgar, P. Jackson, Manson (manager); Prescott, Mitchell (manager), Ashton, Whiteley, Huddart; Front: Harris, Ackerley, Murphy, Pitchford.
(Photo: Courtesy Robert Gate)

Manson readily agreed, but Mitchell took a little time before giving his consent. It was left to Manson to find a suitable location. By all accounts it was Eddie Waring who proposed Surfers' Paradise, a developing beach resort 50 miles away, as the place to go. Manson made the arrangements and was ridiculed in the Australian press for it. When the squad got back from tour matches in north Queensland, the Test team, which included a fit again Sully, plus two reserves were picked and despatched to the coast for four days special training.

The party returned to Brisbane on Saturday morning. Later that day, Sully, at 24, was the oldest member of Great Britain's youngest ever backline which took the field at the Exhibition Ground behind a pack that contained three new caps – Dick Huddart, Vince Karalius and Brian McTigue. It was undoubtedly a high risk selection, but crucially Brough had struck the right balance of craft, pace and power in the pack. The British team was Eric Fraser; Ike Southward, Eric Ashton, Jim Challinor, Mike Sullivan; Dave Bolton, Alex Murphy; Alan Prescott, Tommy Harris, Brian McTigue, Dick Huddart, Johnny Whiteley, Vince Karalius.

There was a major setback to Britain's hopes when Alan Prescott's forearm was badly injured in a tackle after just four minutes. While

Prescott was taking stock of his injury, Jim Challinor surprisingly scored Great Britain's first try to put the Lions in the lead. Just over 10 minutes later, after Sully had failed to make the most of a pass from his stand-off, Dave Bolton was caught late and suffered a broken collar bone. Bolton had to leave the field, reducing Great Britain to 11 fit men. Vince Karalius had to be pulled out of the pack to play at stand-off and Sully was forced to provide emergency cover in the centre. Two penalty goals from Eric Fraser pushed the Lions further ahead before Sully got a try on 34 minutes, following good work by Alex Murphy and Brian McTigue. This gave the Lions a 10–2 lead that they held up to half-time.

Back in the dressing room the severity of Prescott's arm injury was assessed. A break was confirmed and Prescott was told by the doctor not to return to the field. For the good of his team Prescott decided to return to the fray and everyone in the dressing room agreed to keep his injury a secret.

Sticking to their game plan, the Lions came out after the break determined to play attacking rugby. It paid off when, within a couple of minutes Ike Southward had crossed for a try which was converted by Eric Fraser. Halfway through the half, Southward got a second and again Fraser converted. Although Australia fought back and closed the gap, Great Britain held the lead throughout and thanks to a late try from Alex Murphy won a historic and dramatic match 25–18.

The series had been squared and the Ashes were still there for the taking. But a high price had been paid for victory. Four players – Dave Bolton, Jim Challinor, Alan Prescott and Vince Karalius – were taken to hospital and for two of them, Dave Bolton and Alan Prescott, their tour was over.

Sully missed the final match in Queensland, against Toowoomba on Wednesday 9 July, and the one against North Coast NSW at Lismore on Sunday 13 July.

Special training, having worked once, was repeated before the third test. After the mayhem of Brisbane three changes had to be made – Alan Prescott was replaced by Abe Terry, Dave Bolton by Phil Jackson and Jim Challinor by Alan Davies. In Prescott's absence, Phil Jackson took over as captain. Tom Mitchell and Jim Brough assembled their squad of 15 and headed off to Cronulla, 30 miles away, for four days.

There was much to be done to get a much changed team ready to face Australia at the SCG on Saturday 19 July.

With so much at stake, both teams struggled to gain the upper hand in front of another huge crowd of 68,720. Over the first 40 minutes the teams seemed almost equally matched and it was no surprise at half-time that the Lions held a slender advantage, 14–12. When play resumed the Lions took control. Sully scored two tries in the run up to the hour to put the game out of Australia's reach. The large crowd expressed its anger and frustration as the Australian team failed to match the British and bombarded the pitch with fruit, bottles and other rubbish. After Sully was awarded his second try midway through the second half, which was disputed because of an earlier alleged obstruction, he and the referee became the targets for the bombardment.

What happened next was described by Eddie Waring, who was covering the match as a journalist: "When Sullivan returned to the Sydney Hill end of the ground all hell broke loose. The bottle, orange and apple bombardment started in full force. Then 'Sully' struck.

Coolly, calmly, cheekily, he picked up an orange. And as the missiles whizzed about him he peeled it – then ate it! The crowd went mad. But 'Sully' hadn't finished yet.

He then picked up a bottle, took off the top, and drank the contents. Every single drop. The crowd roared and roared to the end of the match. 'Sully' didn't worry. Neither did his team mates. Britain won by 40 points to 17 points – and with it the Ashes."

Sully went on to grab the Lions' seventh try, a length of the field effort, on 76 minutes to complete a record win over Australia. In doing so, Sully had become only the fifth Briton to have scored a hat-trick in an Ashes test match. He was also the last to record one. The Lions had triumphed and retained the Ashes in Australia for the first time since 1946. Their first priority had been achieved and now it was time for them to move on. They packed and departed for Auckland the following day.

Sully missed the opening match in New Zealand against the Maori at Huntly on Wednesday 23 July, but retained his place in the Great Britain team that took on New Zealand three days later. After the superb performance in Sydney the week before the Lions were disappointing on a heavy pitch in Auckland.

Mick in test match action in Australia in 1958.
(Photo: Courtesy *Rugby League Journal*)

Injuries blighted the selection and meant that an unfit Vince Karalius had to play because there were no other fit forwards available. The Lions fell behind early before a Pitchford break provided the opening for Sully to get over the line and cut the Kiwis' lead to 10–5. That was as good as it got and New Zealand won 15–10 to go one up in the series.

Possibly the worst aspect of the New Zealand leg of the tour was the almost constant travelling that was necessary to ensure that each of the game's centres got a chance to see the Lions. Sully was one of 15 fit players who left Auckland airport on Monday bound for New Plymouth where they played Taranaki. It proved a very easy match. Sully ran in six tries in a 67–8 victory. On Tuesday, having been joined by the rest of the party, they flew on to Wellington before taking on the local XIII the following day. It was another easy win; Sully collected three tries as the Lions won 62–20.

Dissent was brewing among the players and it broke out into the open in Wellington. The players passed a vote of 'no confidence' in Jim Brough and produced a letter signed by all 21 of them which was passed to Tom Mitchell for him to forward to the RL Council. Mitchell asked for the matter to remain secret while the tour progressed and the players respected that wish.

The next day, Thursday, the party took to the air once more for the journey to Christchurch. There they enjoyed the luxury of a day off before meeting Canterbury on Saturday. Eight of the 23 players were carrying injuries so Sully was called upon to play his fourth match in eight days. Canterbury proved to be stronger opposition and reached the break 14–8 ahead. However, injuries forced the home side to reshuffle their backs and the Lions took advantage. Sully was in fine form; he scored three tries and had one disallowed as the Lions went on to win comfortably, 41–21.

Immediately after the match against Canterbury, the whole tour party set off by train for the west coast of the South Island and arrived just after midnight. After an early training session they met West Coast at Greymouth on Sunday 3 August. Conditions were so cold and wet that the teams agreed to turn round immediately at half-time and not take a break. Although he did not score, Sully had a couple of front teeth loosened in a hard physical game which the Lions won 19–2.

The following day, the fittest players, one of whom was Sully, were selected to play against Combined Provinces, and sent by plane to Palmerston North. A mounting injury list meant Sully had to turn out at scrum-half against a weak combined side at The Showground on Wednesday 6 August. The Lions outclassed the locals and won 72–3, to equal their biggest ever victory margin in New Zealand. After half-an-hour, Sully touched down to add a try to the Lions' total, which would finally reach 18.

The following day the team returned to Auckland where the rest of the party were waiting ahead of the second test against New Zealand which was to be played at Carlaw Park on Saturday 9 August. It was a match the Lions had to win if the series was to be squared.

Facing the final test, the Lions rediscovered their form, none more so than Sully who scored a hat-trick. His first try came from an Eric Ashton break early in the first half. The second was again set up by Ashton after only a minute of the second half, Sully scoring under the posts to put the Lions' back in front. The third and best saw Sully capitalise on an opening created by Dick Huddart to run in from 70 yards to once again regain the advantage for Great Britain. The Lions finally won 32–15 to square the series.

However, Sully's left ankle was injured touching down for his second try and he was not able to play against the country's most powerful province, Auckland, two days later, in what was the traditional finale of the New Zealand leg of the tour. Victory over Auckland completed the New Zealand itinerary and the Lions returned to Sydney on Tuesday.

Having been declared fit, Sully was selected to play against Sydney Colts at the SCG two days later. It was an ill-starred return. Sully was injured by the first tackle he received and as a passenger for the rest of the match was unable to contribute much to a 19–11 win. His injured left ankle meant he was not available to play in the final match on the eastern seaboard, against Coalfields at Maitland.

As planned, 12 members of the party flew home (a 13th, Ken Jackson had gone home in late June) from Sydney on Wednesday 20 August. Sully made a case to be among them, but in the end he went on with the rest to Perth. All of Great Britain's remaining 14 players who went on to Perth were weary and many were carrying injuries. With Jim Challinor virtually a passenger all the other 13 had to play.

Tom Mitchell tells a story in his memoirs about Sully and the build up to that final match. "He was an ambitious, even obsessive try scorer, and the (tour) try scoring record was achievable if only I could get him to Perth, even on one leg. He needed five tries. 'We will take the play to you, no need to be moving about a lot – the final pass will reach you and all you have to do is hop. 'No can do.' But a few more mentions of the magic word 'record' and with a fixed gleam in his eye he was on the plane to Perth. He hopped over for the record and was a very happy player indeed – having notched up seven tries – two more than required."

That final match took place at the WACA in Perth on Sunday 24 August. It was not quite as straightforward as anticipated. Injuries meant that Sully, with an injured ankle, had to play more centrally at stand-off. But as Mitchell says, once on the field, Sully forgot about the injury and concentrated on the task in hand. He crossed the try line seven times to set a new record for a British player on tour in Australia. Victory, 69–23, also meant the Lions had gone through the tour unbeaten by a non-test team.

Sully and the rest of the tour party set off for home on Wednesday 27 August. He had played in 19 matches out of 30 and scored 38 tries, to beat Billy Boston's record, set four years earlier, by two. The Lions had every right to be proud. They had won a record number of matches, 27, put a record score on the board at the SCG and played before some near record crowds. Once the accounts had been completed the tour's profit could be calculated. Of that profit, 30 per cent went to the players, which gave Sully a tour bonus of £567.

Sully during his time at Wigan.

Fighting for the ball at Wigan.

10. More success with Wigan

With probably the strongest squad in the league, much was expected of Wigan in the 1958–59 season. Joe Egan's men had a lot to live up to, but with Sully and South African full-back Fred Griffiths available for a full season for the first time, Egan had more scoring power at his disposal than ever before.

Shrugging off the effects of a long summer tour and the tiredness from a long journey home, Sully and his three tour-mates immediately reclaimed their places in the Wigan first-team. Only 12 hours after touching down at Heathrow, they were running out at Swinton in a Lancashire Cup first round tie on Saturday 30 August. Under such circumstances it was hardly surprising that Sully did not get on the scoresheet as Wigan claimed a satisfying 37–12 victory.

None of the summer tourists were chosen by the Yorkshire selectors when they met on Thursday 4 September to pick the team to play against Cumberland on Monday 15 September, so Sully missed out.

For Wigan, hopes were high that the Lancashire Cup would find its way to Central Park this season, but first a difficult trip to Oldham for a second round tie on the evening of Tuesday 16 September had to be negotiated. In a tense first half the Oldham defence proved up to the task and the teams went in at half-time level at 4–4. Immediately after the resumption, Wigan took the lead and it looked like Sully had increased it further, but his try was disallowed for a forward pass. After that Oldham struck back and eventually won 19–7. Wigan's hopes of early silverware were dashed. Despite their success in other competitions, Wigan often struggled in the Lancashire Cup. After winning it in 1951–52, their next success was in 1966–67.

Having failed to score in the 46–5 thrashing of Featherstone Rovers on the Saturday, Sully returned to scoring ways for Yorkshire against Lancashire at Craven Park, Hull on Wednesday 24 September. Following defeat at Whitehaven against Cumberland, the Yorkshire selectors had made sweeping changes to their team. Only two backs, Frank Dyson and Jeff Stevenson, were retained. Sully was recalled and was the only tourist to be included.

Facing four of his Wigan team mates, Sully scored two tries in an emphatic 35–19 win. Each county had won one match in the Championship, Yorkshire finishing as runners up on points difference.

To decide a champion, a play-off between the two counties with the best record – Lancashire and Yorkshire – was arranged.

Although Sully scored a try, Wigan lost 17–8 at Headingley on the Saturday before the County play-off. Both sets of selectors had stayed as loyal as they could to the teams that had played one month earlier – Yorkshire made two changes and Lancashire just one. Having finished top, Lancashire got home advantage, at Hilton Park, Leigh, for the decider on Wednesday 29 October. Played under floodlights, Sully scored two tries in a 16–15 win. That one point advantage on the night allowed Yorkshire to retain the County Championship.

Realising that his first-team chances on the left wing were likely to be few and far between, Terry O'Grady, who had played the first three matches of the season on the right wing, accepted an offer to join Warrington in mid-September. O'Grady's move was the first step in what was to become a significant rearrangement of the Wigan threequarter line. Ernie Ashcroft, who normally played right centre decided to retire in October and to replace him Wigan signed Keith Holden from Leigh for £6,666.

To accommodate the new signing, Eric Ashton, Sully's regular centre partner, moved to right centre, and Keith Holden took over the left-centre position. Holden, a 20-year-old Wiganer with tremendous potential, soon fitted into the threequarter line where he formed a very effective partnership with Sully.

Sully was in superb form at Watersheddings on 20 December. He scored two tries and only being denied two more by some excellent last ditch Oldham defence. Even so Wigan lost 21–18. In front of a capacity Knowsley Road crowd of 29,465 on Boxing Day, Sully got the ball and made a dash for a match saving try as the whistle went, but was denied on the line by Tom van Vollenhoven and Wigan lost 13–9. The following day, Wigan's victory at Leigh marked a change of fortune which would see the club remain undefeated until the start of February.

This season the test series against the French was reduced to two matches. Six months on, virtually the same team that had done battle the previous summer down under once again represented Great Britain against France at Headingley on Saturday 14 March. The team quickly got back into its old form. Sully put the first points on the board with a try after nine minutes. There were four more British tries before half-time, putting the Lions 23–0 up. The interval seemed to break up Great Britain's rhythm and the French managed to close to 26–10 before the Lions regained their concentration. In the last 20 minutes Great Britain ran in six tries – Sully scored two of them (one an obstruction try) – to make the final score 50–15. This was the largest victory margin over the French at that time.

Three weeks later, Sully was one of the 10 players who kept their place in the British team for the return match in France. The test was once again held in Grenoble; the Alpine city was bathed in warm sunshine on match day. There was a total turnaround from the previous encounter and Great Britain went in at the break 19–0 down. A British comeback after the interval could not make up the lost ground and the French won 24–15. This was France's first victory over Great Britain since the matches were granted full test status.

February meant the start of the Challenge Cup and as always Wigan's form and commitment improved. In the league, a Valentine's Day victory at Wilderspool against Warrington marked the start of a real push for a top-four place. The club's defence of the Challenge Cup began one week later. A win over Leeds, 12–5, was followed by another over Hunslet, 22–4, a fortnight later. After those two home ties, Wigan had to travel to Halifax for the next round on Saturday 21 March. Losing the scrums 24–9 should have ended Wigan's Cup hopes, but the visitors positively thrived in those difficult circumstances. Billy Boston scored a hat-trick and Sully contributed two tries as Wigan won 26–0 to progress through to the semi-final.

With a place in the semi-final secured, Wigan's players turned their attention to the league and the need to gain points over Easter to secure a place in the top four. St Helens were already sure of a place which gave their visit to Wigan on Good Friday 27 March even more meaning. The supporters of both clubs certainly thought so as a league record crowd of 47,477, who paid £4,802, packed into Central Park. The home side rose to the occasion and looked set for a comfortable victory, before the Saints rallied and in the end Wigan had to be thankful the visitors lacked a competent goalkicker as they finished 19–14 ahead.

Both the other Easter matches were won as Wigan geared up for six crucial fixtures in April. Five of those were in the league and Wigan won them all. The other was a Challenge Cup semi-final clash with Leigh at Swinton's Station Road on 11 April. Once again Sully scored his side's only try in a very close match which Wigan won 5–0.

In pursuit of the double, Joe Egan took his team over to Blackpool to prepare for the big end-of-season matches. Having finished as Lancashire League champions for the first time since 1951–52 and secured second place in the Northern Rugby League table, Wigan received a visit from third placed Hunslet in the Championship semi-final on Saturday 2 May. The match kicked off late to avoid a clash with the FA Cup Final on television, but it soon became clear that a below full-strength Wigan had thoughts of Wembley in mind. Trailing early in the second half, Wigan put in extra effort to grab the lead, but could not hold on to it and Hunslet went on to win 22–11.

With all hopes of the double shattered, it was back to Blackpool to begin preparations for the Challenge Cup final the following Saturday. A cut knee, which required stitches, sustained in the Hunslet match responded to treatment and Sully was able to take his place again at Wembley on Saturday 9 May. Eric Ashton and John Barton, missing against Hunslet, were back in the team which meant Wigan fielded the same XIII in the final as in all the four earlier rounds of the Cup: Fred Griffiths, Billy Boston, Eric Ashton, Keith Holden, Mick Sullivan, Dave Bolton, Rees Thomas, Bill Bretherton, Bill Sayer, John Barton, Norman Cherrington, Brian McTigue, Roy Evans.

An overawed Hull team offered little threat once Wigan's forwards got the better of their highly rated pack. Having backed up a break by David Bolton, Sully scored a spectacular 75-yard try in the corner to put Wigan 10–2 ahead halfway through the first half. Further tries by Bolton and Boston, both converted by Fred Griffiths, sent Wigan comfortably on the way to a 20–4 lead at the break. Sully almost added another try in the second half, but was unable to ground the ball.

When the final whistle sounded Wigan had won 30–13, to become the first ever club to win successive Wembley finals. Sully's scoring record for Wigan was 27 tries in 41 appearances – 23 from 33 League appearances and four in five Challenge Cup ties. He had failed to score in the Championship play-off match and two Lancashire Cup ties. He also scored seven tries while playing for Yorkshire and Great Britain.

Scoring for Wigan against Leigh in the 1959 Challenge Cup semi-final.
(Photo: Courtesy *Rugby League Journal*)

Winning the Challenge Cup with Wigan at Wembley in 1959.

After collecting his Cup winner's medal and a £50 win bonus Sully's season was over and he was able to take a break from the game after almost three years of constant rugby.

Once the sale of their fish and chip shop was completed, Mick, Jean and two-year old David had left Pudsey. While Sully found work carrying out repairs on council buildings, Jean concentrated on turning a club owned house in the Springfield district of Wigan into a home. In the summer months, Mick took a more serious interest in cricket, joining Billy Boston at the town's Highfield club. He was also able to further his love of horse racing, going to meetings at nearby Aintree and Haydock Park, and became a keen judge of form.

As the players got back into training for the 1959–60 campaign, the simmering discontent over pay threatened to boil over. Wigan's match terms were £10 for a win and £5 for a defeat and the players wanted an increase in losing pay to £7. It might have been expected that the captain, Eric Ashton, or one of the longest serving players, Brian McTigue, would have been nominated to put the players' case to the board. Their choice of spokesman was Sully; the complete professional who could be relied on to put their case forcefully.

Arguing that their team was one of the best paid in the League, the Wigan board offered only an increase in losing pay to £6. That offer was met with the threat of a strike ahead of the public practice match. Negotiations followed and the argument that losing pay was hardly worth the effort if time had to be taken off work seems to have done the trick. Agreement was reached on £7 losing pay but only when significant travel was needed – to matches in the north-west and Yorkshire.

Agreement having been reached, the usual charity opener, the Wardonia Cup match against Warrington, went ahead on 8 August. Wigan won again 31–22. Sully contributed three tries as Wigan made a solid start, taking two wins and a draw from the first four league matches, before the Lancashire Cup began.

Home victories over Rochdale Hornets and Salford offered the prospect of some early Cup success. That was before Warrington proved tougher opponents than expected in the semi-final, held at Central Park on Tuesday 15 September. The lead changed hands a number of times before a last minute Jim Challinor drop-goal knocked out the home side, 15–13. After that loss in the Lancashire Cup, Sully played for Yorkshire the next day against Cumberland at the Boulevard, on Wednesday 16 September, and scored a try in a 26–13 defeat.

Two days after Wigan had lost 18–8 at Rochdale, Sully was again wearing the Yorkshire jersey, this time at York's Clarence Street ground, against the Australians on Monday 28 September. Lancashire had narrowly beaten the Kangaroos the previous week and the Yorkshire team was keen to do the same. They did even better and turned in a dazzling display. Sully contributed one of his side's nine tries as the tourists were thrashed 47–15.

Sully retained his place in a Great Britain XIII that was largely the same as the one which had proved to be so successful the previous year down under for the first test. The match was at Swinton on Saturday 17 October. The terms offered to the players were slightly improved – the fee for a win increasing by £1 to £15 and for a draw by £2 to £10. Losing pay was left unchanged at £8.

Facing the Lions was a much changed Australian team. Only two players, Rex Mossop and Harry Wells, remained from the side beaten in the third test in 1958. Right from the kick-off, the Kangaroos proved too strong for the home side and went in at half-time 12–4 ahead. After conceding an early try in the second half, Great Britain rallied and Sully almost got a try, being forced into touch just a foot short of the line. But the Kangaroos were not to be denied and won 22–14.

Sully would have expected to retain his place in the Yorkshire team to play Lancashire, but that was before a surprising turn of events. During the match at Dewsbury on Saturday 31 October, Sully was cautioned by the referee. When the referee's report was considered at the RFL's disciplinary committee on Tuesday 3 November, its members decided that Sully's actions warranted sterner treatment than a caution and they imposed an unprecedented two match ban, ruling him out of the Wigan team and the Yorkshire team to meet Lancashire on Wednesday 11 November. Without him, Yorkshire still performed superbly to grab a great victory and secure the runner up position behind Cumberland.

Once his suspension was over, Sully was available to take his place for a third encounter with the Australians. This time he was playing for Wigan on Saturday 14 November. Wigan proved too strong for the tourists and won 16–9 to be the fourth club side to beat the Kangaroos.

Tackling one of the Australians for Wigan in 1959.
(Photo: Courtesy Robert Gate)

Tangling with St Helens' Tom van Vollenhoven.
(Photo: Courtesy Robert Gate)

Mick nearly ends up in the crowd against the Australians at Swinton on
17 October 1959. Great Britain lost 22–14.

Mick in action for Great Britain in the third test against the 1959 Australian
tourists at Wigan. Great Britain won 18–12 to take the Ashes.
(Photo: Courtesy *Rugby League Journal*)

Stung into action, the selectors made seven changes in the Great Britain team for the second Test which was held one week later at Headingley. Sully retained his place on the left wing although four other backs did not. The selectors also announced that there would be a more intense build up for the match. Ahead of the usual Thursday get together, two days before the test, the players were instructed to assemble on the Tuesday at Hunslet's Parkside ground. Finally, believing that Gideon Shaw and Jeff Stevenson could not be left to shoulder the entire responsibility of reshaping the team themselves, it was decided to bring in a coach-manager. Surprisingly, instead of choosing an established club coach, the selectors opted to give the job to the RFL's secretary, Bill Fallowfield. They said that he would be present at all the training sessions.

When the team got together on the Tuesday it was discovered that Alan Davies, Sully's regular centre partner against the Australians, had been unable to get time off work and could not take part. As if to indicate the seriousness of the situation, Davies's absence was deemed unacceptable and the selectors called up Eric Ashton to replace him.

It was a tense match, played in muddy conditions that severely restricted open play. Great Britain relied on its pack power, but it appeared that might not be enough as the Kangaroos led 10–6 halfway through the second half. In the build up to the test, Arthur Drewry, writing in the *Yorkshire Post*, had noted how Bill Fallowfield had given special attention to perfecting moves at the play-the-ball and scrum with his captain, Jeff Stevenson. It was one of the latter in the 64th minute that sent loose-forward Johnny Whiteley over for a try, converted by Neil Fox, to seal a narrow win 11–10 which kept the series alive.

The series had been squared, but another victory was needed to retain the Ashes. When the selectors met on Monday 30 November only two team changes were made. They also agreed to leave Bill Fallowfield in charge and continue with an intensive pre-match build up. In the week before the test the players were had to meet at Wigan on the Tuesday before assembling in Southport on the Thursday.

The third test at Central Park on Saturday 12 December was another extremely close match. Once again the British pack eventually got the better of their opposite numbers, but the outcome was in the balance until almost the final whistle. It took a very late try by Ike

Southward to make certain the match went Great Britain's way, 18–12. A very close series had been won by Great Britain and the Ashes had been retained. Thanks to the game's widening horizons, Sully's appearance in the third Test was his 28th cap to equal Alan Prescott's record set between 1951 and 1958. This was the last time that the Ashes were won by Great Britain on British soil.

On the field, Sully was going through a bit of a fallow spell. His try in the draw at Whitehaven on 16 January was his first for the club since one against Liverpool City on 24 October – a run of nine club and two Test matches. Part of that was due to problems at home. Jean gave birth to a daughter, Julie, on 16 February 1960, but she was born with severe health problems, Spina Bifida and a hole-in-the-heart, and only lived for 12 days.

Wigan's campaign to retain the Challenge Cup struggled. As the dying seconds ticked away in the second round tie at Central Park at the end of February, it looked certain that Leeds would be the team to progress, but then Sully dived over in the corner to snatch a win.

On the international stage, a practically unchanged back division was chosen by the selectors for the first test against France at Toulouse on Sunday 6 March. Good work by Jim Drake and Jeff Stevenson set up Sully to score Britain's third try on 23 minutes. The French team were proving the visitors' equals and the Lions reached the break only one point ahead. With 10 minutes remaining, a large brawl led to the dismissal of Derek Turner. Down to 12 men, the British could not hold out and a late try give the home side victory by 20–18.

The following weekend Sully scored a try in Wigan's victory over Oldham. The draw for the third round of the Challenge Cup then sent Wigan over to the Boulevard on 19 March, where the previous year's beaten finalists were determined to put up a much better show. In front of a huge crowd of 25,000, there was little between the two very strong teams. The outcome was in doubt right until the end when a Hull try, two minutes from time, gave the home side a much celebrated 12–8 win. Defeat meant there would be no hat-trick of Wembley victories and no Cup winning bonus for the Wigan players to look forward to later in the spring.

Sully was back on Great Britain duty for the second test against France at St Helens' Knowsley Road on Saturday 26 March. After Neil

Fox had seized upon a French mistake, Sully opened the scoring with a try on 15 minutes. Great Britain had built a 17–7 lead halfway through the second half, but the French were allowed to regain the initiative and were unfortunate not to win. The match ended as a disappointing 17–17 draw.

After an inconsistent start, Wigan finished the season strongly. After a draw at Whitehaven in mid-January, they won 13 of their last 14 matches; the only defeat came at St Helens on Good Friday. Like the club, Sully was on top form and contributed 16 tries during that spell.

Winning all the other seven league matches in April, Wigan overtook a faltering Featherstone Rovers side to grab fourth place in the table. A place in the Championship play-offs brought a short trip to Knowsley Road. On form the Saints, having finished as the league leaders and Lancashire League champions, were clear favourites. They had finished the season 13 points ahead of their greatest rivals and had beaten Wigan both home and away in the league.

Joe Egan, however, had a plan. Sully was chosen to play at stand-off in the Championship semi-final on 7 May. This, said the press, was specifically to close down Alex Murphy who occupied the same position for St Helens. But, as Sully was keen to point out, Wigan had announced its team first so, in his opinion, Saints had actually picked Murphy to mark him.

In front of a crowd of 33,000, Sully went about his job in an abrasive fashion. He had been hit with a couple of stiff-arms before there was one altercation too many with Murphy, which led to both of them being ordered off four minutes before half-time. Saints had been leading 7–2 at that point, but Wigan reorganised. They coped with the loss of a key player better than the home side and won 19–9. Being sent off brought a two match suspension so Sully missed Wigan's victory over Wakefield Trinity in the Championship Final, but he was awarded a Championship medal.

Sully's scoring record for Wigan that season was 26 tries in 38 appearances – 23 of them from his 31 League appearances, one from three Challenge Cup ties and two from three Lancashire Cup ties. He did not score in the Championship play-off. Overall, including representative appearances, he scored 30 tries in the season.

11. A World Cup and a transfer

Sully's suspension still had one match to run so he was forced to miss the Wardonia Cup match on 6 August 1960 and the opening league victory over Barrow at Central Park on Saturday 13 August. Judging by the demolition of Barrow, Wigan had started the 1960–61 season like they finished the last and a further five consecutive league victories seemed to confirm it.

As the County Championship and the World Cup approached, Sully prepared to sign off for Wigan, with a try against Oldham in the first round of the Lancashire Cup on Saturday 27 August. He was in good form for so early in the season and had scored two tries in his four first team appearances. He must have fancied his chances of selection for the World Cup squad. The tournament was due to start on 24 September and run until 8 October in England.

He passed the first stage of the process by retaining his Yorkshire place for the Roses match, which was held at Wakefield Trinity's ground on Wednesday 31 August. With the Tykes in front, it appeared that the game was theirs as they attacked down the left flank. If debutant Terry Clawson had timed his pass correctly, Sully would have had an easy try and Yorkshire would almost certainly have won the match. As it was, Clawson's pass was intercepted and the Red Rose men dashed down the field to score a try. So Lancashire won 21–20.

The World Cup

In August 1957, the International Board (IB) had agreed that the RFL should host the third World Cup tournament. Initially it was expected that it would be in autumn 1961, but then in September 1959 the RFL canvassed support for the tournament to be held in autumn 1960, to link in with the 60th anniversary of the NRL's formation. Although the French had concerns that the new date might have an impact on their performance, coming as it did at the end of their scheduled tour of Australasia, the IB agreed to bring the tournament forward by a year at its meeting in November 1959.

The season had only been underway for four weeks before the RFL started its build up for the World Cup with a trial at St Helens on the evening of Monday 12 September. Sully appeared for an England XIII which beat the Rest of the League 21–16 in front of a crowd of 13,500.

Two days later, Sully played in a largely unchanged Yorkshire team against Cumberland at Whitehaven's Recreation Ground. Sully capitalised on two Jeff Stevenson inspired breaks to score two tries, but Yorkshire could not cope with having to play for the whole of the second half without Harold Poynton and crashed to a third successive defeat in Cumberland, 43–19. A second defeat meant Yorkshire were definitely going to finish at the bottom of the table.

The selection committee had announced an 18-man British squad, which included only eight forwards, earlier that same day. As was so often the way with trials, the final squad was comprised of 10 men from the Great Britain team, five from the Rest and three, who for one reason or another, had not played in that match. There were four Wigan players in the squad – Eric Ashton, Billy Boston, Brian McTigue and Sully.

The terms being offered for the tournament were improved, but hardly generous – £20 for a win, £13 for a draw and £10 for a defeat – plus a bonus of £25 if Great Britain finished as world champions. While the tournament was underway, the league programme was effectively suspended and the players were not available to play for their clubs. Sully's last match for Wigan before the tournament was in a 14–2 defeat at Whitehaven on Thursday 17 September.

Bill Fallowfield, Great Britain's team manager, was left to fashion a team out of the squad when the players assembled at Hunslet's Parkside ground for training three days before the opening match. Billy Boston's injury, which had ruled him out of the trial, was still causing him problems and Great Britain's management waited anxiously for good news. Despite the sidelining of a potential match winner, the British team were rated as favourites, although both Australia and New Zealand were coming to Britain after hard home series against the touring French side.

The tournament began for Great Britain with a match against New Zealand at Odsal Stadium on Saturday 24 September. In the build up to the match, the Kiwis' coach, Travers Hardwick, had threatened to catch the home team unawares. Yet, on a perfect day for rugby league, the Kiwis, despite fielding their strongest XIII, failed to do themselves justice after a month's lay-off.

82

The 1960 World Cup squad.
(Photo: Courtesy Robert Gate)

Mick getting away from New Zealand's Tom Hadfield at Odsal
on 24 September 1960. Great Britain won 23–8.
(Photo: Courtesy Robert Gate)

The Lions took most of the first half to find their rhythm, but played better after the break and went on to record a comfortable opening victory, 23–8. The tournament was played on a league basis, and on the same day Australia beat France 13–12 at Wigan.

One week later, Great Britain met France at Swinton. It had been hoped that Billy Boston would be fit for this match, but he still was not available and this time Jim Challinor had to fill in on the right wing. With a couple of changes in the pack, the British team performed much better in this match. Just before the break, Brian McTigue and Vince Karalius worked a try for Sully out wide to send the Lions into the dressing rooms 13–7 ahead. After their exertions the previous week against Australia, the French tired in the second half and Great Britain recorded another comfortable win, 33–7. Australia beat the Kiwis 21–15 at Headingley.

With two wins to their credit, it was back to Hunslet for the Lions ahead of their third and final match. This was the last World Cup tournament not to end with a final, so the match against a similarly undefeated Australia at Bradford was for the title. Billy Boston was finally fit and he was brought in on the right wing to face an Australian team that was largely the same as the one that had pushed the Lions so close in the Ashes series a year earlier.

A very wet and muddy Odsal Stadium was the dismal scene for a crucial encounter. A crowd of 32,773 was present. Having won the toss, the Lions opted to play with the rain and wind at their backs. On a day made for forward play, Great Britain's pack proved decisive. Instead of a spectacle, the match degenerated into a nasty, vicious clash that turned into mass brawls on a couple of occasions. Sully was flattened and left concussed midway through the first half. Despite his injury, he still managed to back up a break by Alex Murphy and run in a try from 35 yards 10 minutes before half-time which, with the conversion, put Britain ahead, 10–0. Sully had no recollection of this try after the match, probably as a result of some rough treatment handed out by the Australian second-row forward, Elton Rasmussen. After the break, facing the elements, the British defence took control and restricted the Kangaroos to just a late try, to secure victory and the trophy with a 10–3 win. At Central Park, 2,876 fans saw New Zealand beat France 9–0.

Despite suffering concussion, Sully was back on the field for Great Britain against a Rest of the World XIII, at Odsal Stadium, two days later. Concussed or not, he made his presence felt and scored one of the game's 16 tries, to help the Lions to a 33–27 win.

When the tournament began Sully had made 31 successive international appearances for England and Great Britain. His three appearances in the World Cup meant that he had equalled fellow Wigan start Ken Gee's record of 34 appearances for those two countries set between 1946 and 1952.

The World Cup tournament over, the Wigan contingent returned to Central Park and the league programme restarted. Sully scored two tries in a 17–15 defeat at the hands of Leigh, at Central Park, on Saturday 15 October. One week later, he was back at stand-off for the visit to Knowsley Road. This time there were no fireworks or dismissals. Allowed a little more space, Alex Murphy proved how much of a threat he could pose and scored two tries, as Saints won 11–6.

Just two months after being crowned world champions, the British team had to put its reputation on the line once more. Sully was one of nine members of the World Cup winning team who retained their places for the first of the annual encounters with France. The match was at the Stade Municipal in Bordeaux on Sunday 11 December. It was a tough hard encounter. Despite having only limited possession, the Lions still managed to run in four second half tries to secure a merited 21–10 win.

Back at Central Park, Joe Egan's plans, which seemed to be working so well when the season started, now seemed to have gone awry. The champions were struggling on the field and in a bid to get back to winning ways Egan transfer-listed a number of players over the first half of the season and went in search of new blood. One of his more interesting acquisitions was St Helens' tourist winger, Frank Carlton, who had lost his first team place to the South African Jan Prinsloo.

To accommodate Frank Carlton, who had cost the club a £5,000 fee, Sully was moved to left centre and Keith Holden to right centre for the visit to Hunslet on 5 November. Whether this reorganisation was intended as permanent is doubtful because two weeks later Keith Holden was on his way to Oldham.

Mid-December saw a bout of influenza swept through the club's ranks. A number of players were affected; Sully was one along with Billy Boston and Brian McTigue. None of them made the trip to Workington on Christmas Eve, but Sully discovered that Boston and McTigue had been paid whereas he had not. When told that was because they were fit and he was not, he was angry. He subsequently missed the home match against Salford on Boxing Day.

The New Year did not start off too well. Sully got caught up in traffic and arrived at Central Park only five minutes before kick-off for the match against Warrington on Monday 2 January. Unimpressed, Joe Egan replaced him and made him back reserve. He was back in the first team, in the centre, the following Saturday at Swinton, 7 January, for what was his last appearance for Wigan. Behind the scenes there was tension. Sully let it be known that "I have not been paid at all since Christmas – not even for the Warrington match when I was a reserve. I have seen the directors twice about pay and got nowhere." His request for a transfer was accepted by the board on Monday 9 January and the fee was set at £11,000.

Wakefield Trinity were said to be prepared to renew their interest from the previous season, but in the end the Sullivans did not want to leave Lancashire or, more specifically, their new home of just four months on Ravenhead Drive in Upholland with its view of Ashurst Beacon. Mick also had a new job, working as an agent, alongside Fred Griffiths, for a Wigan insurance firm.

Although St Helens had reputedly splashed out £7,500 to secure John Tembey from Whitehaven the previous week, just four days after Sully was put on the transfer list, Harry Cook, the Saints chairman announced his signing. Jack Wood had done a good job on Wigan's behalf. He secured a fee of £11,000, a new record, and more importantly, a profit of £1,500 after three years great service. From a St Helens viewpoint, club historian Alex Service said that the recruitment of Sullivan, "arguably the greatest post-war left winger of them all" was a "sensational" move by the club.

Sully's move promoted a brief flurry of high spending on the transfer market. Later that week, Saints recouped some of that outlay by transferring Jan Prinsloo to Wakefield Trinity, who paid a club record £9,000 for his services. The new record fee for Sully stood for just five days before Workington Town broke it by signing Ike Southward from

Oldham for £11,002/10; the extra £2/10 (£2.50) being the price in those days of a bottle of whisky.

Sully's scoring record for Wigan in 1960–61 was seven tries in 16 appearances – six from 15 appearances in the league and one from a Lancashire Cup tie. In total, Sully had made 125 appearances for Wigan: 104 on the wing, 18 at centre and 3 at stand-off. He scored 84 tries for 252 points.

Jack Winstanley reflected on Sully's time at Central Park in his *Illustrated History* of the club: "…He was worth the fee paid by Wigan and pound for pound (weight, that is) [was] the hardest player I ever saw. Mi9ck Sullivan, to say the least, was volatile. Some of his tackling was murderous, almost devilish in its intensity, and his disciplinary record shows that it wasn't always fair. Yet he didn't weigh more than 11 stones and I never saw him measure up the opposition before wading in. At best he was a supreme winger who scored some superb tries by dint of sure handling, exquisite timing and fearless execution."

St Helens

Once again Sully found himself following in Jim Sullivan, his famous namesake's, footsteps. During his time at the club as coach, Jim Sullivan had turned the Saints into a major force – bringing both the Championship and the Challenge Cup to Knowsley Road. However, in 1959 he had announced he would leave the club when his seven-year contract came to an end. Besides winning trophies, Jim Sullivan had built up a core of world class players – Tom van Vollenhoven, Alex Murphy, Dick Huddart and Vince Karalius – at Knowsley Road.

It was a huge task to find a coach to succeed a legend like Jim Sullivan and the Saints board decided to promote from within. Sully's former Great Britain captain, Alan Prescott, was given the chance to translate his superb on-field leadership into a coaching role, initially as captain-coach. Harnessing the talent on the club's roster was a big challenge, especially for someone like Prescott who was taking his first steps in coaching. In Prescott's defence, there were signs of progress, especially after a successful campaign in the Lancashire Cup earlier in the season.

Although he was Great Britain's test left winger, it was at right centre that Sully made a try scoring debut for St Helens, in a 22–15 victory over Hull at Knowsley Road, on 16 January. Maybe the Saints selectors knew something, for Sully duly appeared in the centre for Great Britain in the return match against France at Knowsley Road on Saturday 28 January. There was a moment of comedy when Sully was wrongly cautioned by the referee for a high tackle which had been committed by his new team mate Vince Karalius. The British team was never really troubled and won comfortably, 27–8.

It took a replay in the first round of the Challenge Cup for Saints to beat local rivals Widnes; after a draw at Knowsley Road on 11 February, the Saints won the replay 29–10 at Naughton Park. Saints went on to beat Castleford 18–10 in the second round at Wheldon Road on Saturday 25 February.

Having helped the Saints successfully, if not convincingly, into the third round draw, Sully got himself sent off and picked up a three match suspension at the start of March. He was forced to miss two league wins and a home victory, thanks to a late rally, over Swinton in the Challenge Cup third round on 11 March. During his enforced absence, the Saints' management gave Johnny Gaydon, a new South African wing recruit, his debut.

When Sully was available for selection once again in mid-March, Gaydon was relegated to the 'A' team as St Helens faced to up the realistic possibility of winning all four Cups, a feat not achieved since 1928. Whether or not they did would depend on how well they dealt with a busy period in late March which would see them play six league matches in 14 days.

It did not go well, the team's form slumped, and as a result Alan Prescott's position came under serious threat. Four defeats around Easter threw everything into doubt, particularly the outcome of the Cup semi-final. It was a slump in form that did Prescott and Sully no favours. One of those defeats came on Good Friday, 31 March, at his old home ground, Central Park. Now a Saint, Sully was part of a team that failed to rise to the occasion and lost 12–2 in front of another huge crowd of 42,899.

Defeat in so many league matches ahead of the semi-final panicked the Saints board who made an approach to Jim Brough about joining the club temporarily as a backs coach. News of this reached the Saints squad through the grapevine and they unanimously passed a "vote of no confidence in such an appointment". This news was conveyed to the board in a letter whose first signatory was the captain Vince Karalius and the second was Mick Sullivan. In total the letter carried the signatures of 28 players. It was an impressive show of loyalty to Prescott and the board had no choice but to drop the idea.

The first Saturday in April took the Saints over to Hull in a dress rehearsal for the Challenge Cup semi-final. Saints pulled themselves together to secure a morale boosting win at the Boulevard, which confirmed them as favourites for their meeting one week later. To get ready for that match, an injury hit Saints' team stayed at Ilkley and from there travelled to Odsal for a meeting with Hull FC, who were looking for a third successive Wembley appearance. Before an all-ticket crowd of 42,074 on Saturday 15 April, Saints fought hard for a 5–4 half-time lead. After the break it was a different story as Saints rediscovered their winning ways and ran in five tries to win convincingly 29–6. It had been a hard fought win during which Sully had insisted on returning with a head wound that required six stitches after the match. In the other semi-final, Wigan beat Halifax 19–10 at Station Road.

Their poor form had cost the Saints the Lancashire League and seen them fall to fourth in the NRL table. At least they had managed to qualify for the Championship play-offs, which meant a trip to Headingley to meet a top-of-the-table Leeds team on 6 May. As this was their first meeting that season, Leeds were something of an unknown quantity. On the day, the Loiners were always in front and Sully could only grab hold of Wilf Rosenberg's ankles as the winger dived in for his second – and the home side's third – try to complete an 11–4 victory.

Ahead of the meeting with their greatest rivals on the game's greatest stage, Saints trained at Southport. In view of Saints' recent poor league form, Wigan were the favourites. Sully was determined to play even though he had a slightly displaced bone in his foot.

In front of the first capacity crowd for 10 years, who were able to bask in the warm sunshine, Sully faced up to his recent Wigan teammates at Wembley on Saturday 13 May. It was a star-studded clash with 14 test players taking part, seven on each side.

Saints with the Challenge Cup in 1961. (Photo: Courtesy Alex Service)

The Saints line up on the day was: Austin Rhodes; Tom van Vollenhoven, Ken Large, Brian McGinn, Mick Sullivan; Alex Murphy, Wilf Smith; Abe Terry, Bob Dagnall, Cliff Watson, Dick Huddart, Don Vines, Vince Karalius.

There was some initial friction between Sully and his former team-mates. Having borne the brunt of a heavy crash tackle in his own in-goal area from Billy Boston, Sully retaliated with a late tackle on his old team-mate. Fortunately, that was the extent of the aggravation and after that Sully and his opposite number and friend could get on with playing rugby.

As predicted, it was a close match, and few try scoring chances came the way of the four star wingers on the field. When half-time arrived, Saints were just ahead, 5–2. Wigan mounted a fight back after the break which almost produced two tries. Then a Wigan handling error was pounced upon by Dick Huddart who fed Ken Large. He sent Tom van Vollenhoven away for a fantastic match-winning try. At the finish, Saints had won 12–6 to earn a welcome £75 win bonus. Victory at Wembley also kept Alan Prescott in a job, at least for the time being.

Writing about a great team effort, Peter Gordon had this to say in the *Reynolds News*: "Sullivan, the former Wigan winger, did not get many attacking chances on the St Helens left flank but he was very sound on defence and the 27-year-old test star adds a third cup medal to the two he gained with Wigan in 1958 and 1959." Having collected another medal the season ended, Sully having scored four tries for St Helens in 19 matches.

Sully in action for St Helens against New Zealand in 1961.
Saints won 25–10. (Photo: Courtesy *Rugby League Journal*)

12. The Kiwis and the Lancashire Cup

Having had the luxury of another long summer break, it was time to get back into action for the 1961–62 season. Pre-season training led up to the usual charity match against Liverpool City, which was held at Knowsley Road on Saturday 12 August. Sully was the only threequarter not to get over the tryline as the Saints won 29–14.

Sully retained his favoured left wing shirt for the opening league match, against Leeds on 19 August. He scored a try as Saints got the new season underway in style with a 20–5 home win. He kept hold of that shirt for the following match at Swinton, but appeared at left centre in the first round of the Lancashire Cup, scoring a try in a 43–8 thrashing of Leigh.

After a gap of six years, a young and enthusiastic Kiwi party was back in Britain for a full tour. They proved to be an unexpected handful for many of the British teams they met. Sully was called up by the Yorkshire selectors for the match against the Kiwis at Craven Park, Hull on Wednesday 6 September. After winning just two of their opening five matches against scratch club combinations, the Kiwis were obviously struggling and Yorkshire won 21–11.

Back in action for the Saints on the following Saturday, Sully failed to score at Salford as the Saints won comfortably 24–7. Despite having had the advantage of a run out against the Kiwis, the Yorkshire team, with just a couple of changes, lost heavily, 23–8, to Cumberland at Wakefield two days later.

Sully was surprisingly omitted from the test team when the selection committee met on Wednesday 20 September. That decision ended a run of 35 consecutive test appearances stretching back to 1954, and two 'unofficial' tests. His replacement was Warrington and Lancashire's Terry O'Grady who had been the last man to wear the number 5 jersey in a test match before Sully had practically made it his own over seven years ago. Alfred Drewry writing in the following day's *Yorkshire Post* commented that "Sullivan, at 28, should now be in his prime, but in the last season or two he has lost some pace, and his sidestep has not the flickering quality which used to be the terror of opposing full-backs."

Instead of turning out in a Great Britain shirt at Headingley on Saturday 30 September, Sully was on duty at Knowsley Road where

Hull inflicted a surprise 25–22 defeat on the home side. In many ways Sully was fortunate to miss what turned into an emphatic first test defeat for the Lions. The Kiwis won 29–11 in front of a 16,540 crowd.

A month had passed before Yorkshire played its second match in the County Championship. By then, Cumberland had also beaten Lancashire to claim the title. Therefore this year's war of the roses encounter, at Leigh's Hilton Park on Monday 9 October, would be to determine which county finished bottom of the table. Yorkshire's selectors had rung the changes, eight in all, but the rebuilt team was not quite strong enough and Sully's final appearance for the county ended in a 14–12 defeat. So Yorkshire retained the wooden spoon.

In response to that first test setback, the selection committee at its meeting on Tuesday 10 October made seven team changes for the second Test. Sully was recalled in place of Terry O'Grady in the British line up. Alfred Drewry was hardly impressed commenting that "Sullivan ... can count himself lucky that there is a dearth of outstanding left wingers". Sully's recall meant there were a record five Saints – the others being Bob Dagnall, Dick Huddart, Alex Murphy and Abe Terry – in the British team. It was too much of an honour for St Helens who immediately applied and received approval to postpone their meeting with Swinton scheduled for the test weekend.

At the end of the week, Sully was back facing the Kiwis, just a week before the second test. This time he was playing for St Helens, one of only six clubs that had been given standalone fixtures against the tourists. On seven occasions, the tourists faced combinations such as the two Hull clubs, Oldham and Rochdale Hornets, and Leeds, Bramley and Hunslet. The Kiwis showed plenty of respect for their hosts, and fielded practically their test team at Knowsley Road on Saturday 14 October. Although Sully did not manage to get on the scoresheet, the Saints won comfortably, 25–10, in front of a 21,680 crowd.

In a bid to ensure that the series was squared, the selection committee decided that more thorough preparation was needed. It was agreed that the team would assemble three days before the next test and train at Hunslet's Parkside ground on the Wednesday and Thursday. Sully joined a group of players who were hardly happy about the match fee. As one disgruntled unnamed St Helens' player (quite possibly Sully) told Eddie Waring "£15 is not enough. We got that sum as a club for beating New Zealand."

Mick leaping over a teammate for Great Britain against New Zealand in 1961.
(Photo: Courtesy *Rugby League Journal*)

It had been a rather lacklustre season so far for Sully. He had only scored four tries in 11 appearances for Saints, but in this test, held at Odsal Stadium on Saturday 21 October, he answered his critics and showed once more what a big match player he was. The game did not start well for Great Britain; the Kiwis took an early lead through a converted try. The home side needed a score and Sully provided it with a try just before the half hour. Five minutes later he got a second as he touched down an Alex Murphy kick through. Although both were too wide out to be converted, with a couple of Neil Fox penalty goals they sent the British team in at half-time 10–5 ahead. Sully did not manage to score after the break, but Great Britain went on to square the series with a 23–10 win.

Great Britain made only one change, in the pack, for the third test at Swinton two weeks' later. With the outcome of the series resting on this match, the British team was taken over to Southport for three days special preparation. Two penalties once again gave New Zealand an early lead, which was soon overcome. Sully scored Great Britain's third and fourth tries to help the home side build an 18–6 lead at half-time. After the break, the British team maintained its form. They passed the 30-point mark with 17 minutes remaining to top Wigan's score against the tourists and secure a gold watch each from Mackeson. The Kiwis never stopped trying and scored two late tries to make the match look closer than it really was. After the initial setback at Headingley Great Britain had recovered well to win the series 2–1.

The Lancashire Cup had again proved kind to the Saints who progressed through to the final with comfortable victories over Leigh, Oldham and Salford. An injury hit Swinton provided the opposition in the final at Central Park on Saturday 11 November, the week after the third test. The Lions put up a strong showing and only trailed 9–4 at the break. Not long into the second half, one of Swinton's props was dismissed and the unequal contest proved too much for the Lions. Saints took full advantage and ran in a further four tries to retain the trophy and provide Sully with his first Lancashire Cup winner's medal.

Their Lancashire Cup run was in sharp contrast to a very disappointing league campaign; Saints were consistently inconsistent. After the celebrations at Swinton, they lost five of their next seven league matches. By mid-December the situation was becoming critical.

St Helens – Lancashire Cup winners in 1961. Back: Fred Leyland, Dick Huddart, Bob Dagnall, Vince Karalius, Cliff Watson, Ray French, Wilf Smith; front: Brian McGinn, Alex Murphy, Ken Large, Mick Sullivan, Austin Rhodes, Tom van Vollenhoven. (Photo: Courtesy *Rugby League Journal*)

Having called off a couple of matches and skipped a few training sessions due to injuries and business commitments, Vince Karalius was stripped of the captaincy. That did not have the desired effect, and a home defeat by Oldham proved the final straw for the Saints' board. A change of coach was called for and Alan Prescott was ousted on 19 December. The Saints' board promoted another former playing favourite, Stan McCormick, the reserve team trainer, as Prescott's successor, initially on a temporary basis.

Having taken charge, McCormick cracked the whip. The senior players seem to have been the prime targets and Sully was informed that he had been dropped on the day before the visit of Warrington, on Saturday 20 January. Upset and angry at the decision, Sully told reporters on the Friday evening that he was seeking a meeting with club officials and that if there was not a satisfactory outcome he would consider retiring so that he could concentrate on his career in insurance.

The first signs of the disillusionment that would blight the rest of his time at Knowsley road were becoming apparent. On that same Friday, Vince Karalius, who had also threatened to retire to concentrate on his business interests, was placed on the transfer list.

After years of often intense argument, the NRL had agreed to return to a two division format, last used over 50 years ago, and this season's final league positions would determine which one would be home to the Saints in 1962/63. Only a top–16 finish would guarantee First Division rugby at Knowsley Road and McCormick had little choice but to start making changes as he attempted to discover a winning blend.

McCormick attempted to raise fitness levels and encourage a more open style of play, but Saints continued to be unpredictable. Sully had patched up his differences with the club's officials and returned to first team action against Huddersfield in a league match at Knowsley Road on 3 February. Saints were in sparkling form and the visitors' defence was unable to cope with them. Sully helped himself to five of Saints' eight tries in a 36–5 rout of his old club. Yet, four weeks later, the same two clubs met again at Knowsley Road in the second round of the Challenge Cup and this time Huddersfield, the eventual finalists, beat practically the same Saints' team 13–2 to end any hopes of keeping the trophy in St Helens.

The RFL's international committee had announced in December that no tour trial matches for the forthcoming Australia and New Zealand tour would be held. Obviously, the series win against New Zealand and the upcoming series against France were thought to provide enough of a form guide, which appeared to make Sully an automatic choice for the tour as the incumbent left winger.

There appears to have been a view at the RFL that tests against France did not justify preparation time. With an eye on the upcoming tour, the selectors looked to youth and chose an experimental pack, including three debutants, for the first test against France at Wigan on Saturday 17 February. Being experimental still did not warrant any kind of get together and the players met for the first time in Central Park's dressing room one hour before kick-off.

Sully deals with a Widnes player as Tom van Vollenhoven looks on.
(Photo: Courtesy *Rugby League Journal*)

Sully missed Salford's visit to Knowsley Road as the British team took on the French. A flowing passing move involving Terry Clawson, Abe Terry, Barry Simms, Dave Bolton and Neil Fox produced a try for Sully on 32 minutes that put Britain into a strong position, 13–2 ahead. After the break, the inexperienced British team struggled in the face of a strong French fightback and the visitors went on to gain their first ever test victory in England with a 20–15 win.

Sully kept his place for the second test against France which was held at the newly opened Stade Gilbert Brutus in Perpignan three weeks later. A visit to France meant missing another Saints home match, this time against Rochdale Hornets.

The selection committee's decision on tour trials looked even less assured after a Great Britain team, with a much changed pack, again looked out its depth in Perpignan. On a lovely spring afternoon, a poor first half performance against an unchanged French team left Great Britain woefully adrift at the break, 21–5 behind. There was a glimmer of hope when David Bolton worked a move from the first scrum of the second half to set up a try for Sully which reduced the deficit to 21–8. But the deficit was too great and Great Britain slumped to a 23–13 defeat. The team and a dismayed group of selectors arrived back on Monday amid calls for the selection of the tour party to be delayed.

When the Saints had been one of the 20 clubs to vote for the two-division structure, their representatives would have thought it highly unlikely that they could be faced with the drop. But even after defeating Liverpool City 31–7 on Tuesday 13 March they were still in the danger zone, languishing in 15th place with 23 wins and 10 defeats, just two points above what would become a place in the Second Division. Time was running out for Stan McCormick as he struggled to turn the Saints' form around.

Having missed that victory over Liverpool City and then a defeat at Watersheddings, Sully returned to first team duty for the visit of Widnes on Saturday 24 March. For whatever reason, Saints suddenly found their form and won not just that match, but the next five as well. Suddenly, they were moving up and away from the danger zone. The end of that winning run came with the visit of title-chasing Wigan to Knowsley Road on Good Friday. That day, Sully made his last, try scoring, appearance of the season, but it was not enough as a late try gave the visitors victory.

He missed the Saints' last four matches. Without him, they won three of those matches to finally finish ninth. They qualified for the new First Division with nine points to spare. It had not been a vintage season, but Sully had managed to score 15 tries in his 31 appearances for St Helens.

13. The 1962 Lions tour

As widely predicted, Sully was included when the tour squad of 26 was announced as planned on Thursday 22 March. It was an experienced party; Sully was one of the 12 players who had toured previously. Wakefield Trinity's Stuart Hadfield was the manager with Rochdale Hornets' Arthur Walker as his assistant. Colin Hutton, the Hull KR coach, was to accompany the party, but as if to clearly signal that previous tour difficulties would not reoccur, he was announced as merely the trainer.

As in 1958, Sully received the same lump sum, £20, on arrival in Australia and the same £3 per week while on tour. For Jean however, the arrangement was slightly better; she would receive £3/10 (£3.50) each week plus a further £1 per week for David. There would also be a further £10 from St Helens for every test appearance Sully and his teammates, Dick Huddart and Alex Murphy, made on tour.

With just a few days to go before departure it suddenly became clear that the tour would be a little longer than originally planned when the RFL announced that an extra three matches in South Africa would be added at the end of the published itinerary.

Ahead of the 1962 tour, the leading Australian author, Jack Pollard, had compiled a book titled *This is Rugby League*. Sully was one of a number of the game's leading players who contributed articles. As an introduction to Sully's article, Pollard penned this appreciation of his qualities: "Part of the wonder of Mike Sullivan's success has been that he is not a big man (11 stone 12 pounds), but he insists on behaving like one, hurling himself into situations made for giants. Watching him, you are compelled again and again to admire his raw courage, even if occasionally his swinging arms threaten to behead his rivals. Sullivan's tenacity with the ball in his hand, his instinct to be where he can take a try-scoring pass, his speed and opportunism have enabled him to reign for a long time on England's left-wing. Very few chances have come his way since 1953 in Tests that he has not fully exploited. ... He is quick, very quick."

For those who had missed or were too young to remember the 1958 tour, Pollard had certainly painted a picture of a tourist they would not want to miss. And Sully did not disappoint.

Not being involved in the NRL Championship final, Sully was part of the first group of 20 tourists who set off for Perth in Western Australia on Monday 14 May. After a break of nearly a month, Sully was called upon to play in both the opening matches. The first was at the start of the following week against a weak West Australian XIII at Perth where he scored three tries in a 39–12 win for the Lions. After that warm up it was on to Sydney and a midweek match against Riverina at Wagga Wagga. The Riverina men, coached by his old teammate Phil Jackson, were outclassed. Sully scored a try as the Lions won 34–7. By then the rest of the party arrived in Sydney, two days late due to flight delays.

Sully sat out the next couple of matches against Sydney and the trip to Bathurst to face Western NSW, but was back in the Lions' line-up for the match against NSW at the SCG on Saturday 2 June. As it had on a few occasions before, the match against NSW once again turned into a hard, uncompromising encounter. NSW played well but the Lions, with the benefit of a Sully try, ended the first half 23–14 ahead.

Billy Boston and Ken Irvine over on the other wing were sent off 15 minutes into the second half and the huge crowd was at fever pitch. Just as he had been at the same ground four years earlier, Sully was bombarded with fruit and hit on the head by an apple. More worryingly he had been on the receiving end of a sly, but hard punch from his opposite number Mike Cleary. Cleary later recalled how surprised he was that Sully did not flinch, keen to ensure that his opposite number did not realise how badly he had bitten his tongue.

When a brawl erupted following a scrum five minutes from time, both Sully and Cleary raced in as the fracas expanded to embrace everyone on the pitch. When order was restored, the referee had no hesitation in dismissing two front-rowers – Bill Sayer and Billy Wilson – and the remaining two wingers – Cleary and Sully. What had now become a 10-a-side match ended with the Lions in front 33–28.

All those dismissed had their cases heard by the judiciary committee which met a couple of hours later. Once the match was over, Sully had had his tongue wound stitched, but according to Phil King, of the *People*, he and Cleary, who had been wrestling on the ground only a couple of hours earlier, sat together, laughing and joking, as they waited their turn. Their display of mateship cut no ice with the judiciary. Sully, Cleary and both forwards were suspended until the following Tuesday. Boston and Irvine got off with a caution.

The suspension had little effect because as a member of the probable test team, Sully would have remained in Sydney anyway while the rest went north to meet Newcastle where they suffered the first defeat of the tour. After a couple of days rest, Jim Brough's innovation of taking the test team away from the bustle of the city four years earlier was continued – a party of 16 players including Sully, heading off to Coolangatta near Cronulla on Tuesday for two days training prior to the first test.

A week after the match with NSW, the Lions were back at the scene of the battle, the SCG, to meet Australia on Saturday 9 June. Australia shot into an early seven point lead. This seemed to confirm what had been said in the local press in the build up to the match, that the home side were the better team. However, in the end Great Britain triumphed gloriously, 31–12, in a match which passed off without any unpleasant incidents.

Eddie Waring was fulsome in his praise for Sully's performance: "The man who swung the match was Mike Sullivan, hard-bitten veteran of many Tests but never better than on this occasion. His two tries gave Britain the shot in the arm they needed just before half-time." Sully's second try was his eighth in Ashes tests, equalling the Australian, Brian Carlson's record. Disappointed that their hopes had been dashed, the crowd, in scenes reminiscent of the test match four years earlier, pelted apples onto the pitch and Sully picked one up and ate it.

He was one of three test men – the others were Neil Fox and Alex Murphy – who were pressed into service the following day for the match against North Coast NSW at Lismore. The Lions won 33–13, but Sully did not score. After the match it was back to Sydney to pack his bags ready for the flight to Queensland.

Eddie Waring reported in his *Sunday Pictorial* column that before the test win Sully had told him "he was retiring from football when he returns home in August" saying he "wants to finish on top and would like to take the coaching offer" he had received while in Australia.

That was for the future. More immediate was the Monday morning flight north to Brisbane and the start of a three week trek through Queensland with eight matches. Staying at the 93 year old Australian Hotel, the tourists made themselves at home playing Elvis Presley and Chubby Checker records on the juke box. The cost of their entertainment according to Phil King being much reduced when Sully found "a certain lever" at the back of the juke box which returned their sixpences.

Two days later, Sully scored two tries in the floodlit meeting with Brisbane at the Exhibition Ground. Despite his contribution, another defeat seemed on the cards before an Eric Ashton try in the dying seconds rescued the Lions who won 16–14.

The full test line-up was fielded except for Billy Boston and Gerry Round, who were replaced by Eric Fraser and Ike Southward, for the Saturday match against Queensland at Lang Park three days later. Having outplayed the Maroons in a fast-paced first half, the Lions tired and allowed their opponents back into the match after the break and were relieved to finish with a win, 22–17.

After that match, Stuart Hadfield, the tour manager, announced that he was not satisfied with the team's fitness. At times during the second half, the Lions had slowed to almost walking pace. Too much hospitality was taking the edge off his players' fitness and Hadfield told them that something had to be done about it. Derek Turner, the skipper for the day, called a meeting that evening and the players took responsibility for sorting the problem out.

Sully was one of half-a-dozen members of that team spared the 70-mile trip inland to play Toowoomba the next day. Their presence was not missed as the Lions' won comfortably 36–12. When the squad reported for training on Monday morning, the strains of a long tour were beginning to show as another six were placed on the injury list.

Sully returned to action on Wednesday 20 June against Central Queensland under lights at Rockhampton. In hot and humid conditions the Lions won 55–8, but surprisingly Sully's name did not figure among the scorers.

On Friday, Sully was a member of the party that flew north with Stuart Hadfield to take on Far North Queensland at Cairns the following day. All of the team, except Derek Turner, accepted an offer to take a 16 mile boat trip out to Green Island on the Barrier Reef on the morning of the match. On the rough launch trip out, Sully, Frank Carlton and Harold Poynton were very, very ill. According to reports, Sully said he would rather stay on Green Island than face the return trip, but there was no choice, all the party had to go back because they all had to play.

The 1962 Great Britain squad that toured Australia, New Zealand and South Africa. (Photo: Courtesy Robert Gate)

Training in Queensland on tour in 1962.

Sully was only down as a substitute, which was allowed on this tour in matches other than the tests, but he was called on to play. Don Fox's shoulder injury forced him to come off and Sully took over at stand-off. The locals tried hard and the seasick Lions only won in the last minute thanks to a Gerry Round try, converted by Laurie Gilfedder.

It was another full weekend and Sully was called upon to double up against North Queensland at Townsville the following day. Seemingly unaffected by a 240 mile flight, the Lions dominated possession and won comfortably 47–14.

The weekend over, the test squad left for Surfers' Paradise to begin their preparations in a luxury hotel. In the evenings the squad had to make their own entertainment and pictures of Sully and Bill Sayer dressed in hula skirts made the front pages of all the major east coast newspapers. There was a great spirit in the squad and the training sessions set the team up perfectly for the coming test.

The second test, held on Saturday 30 June, marked the debut of Lang Park as a test arena. Injuries to David Bolton and Derek Turner forced two changes to the Lions' line up – Harold Poynton and Laurie Gilfedder were brought in to the side in their place. Despite the loss of those two influential players, the Lions more than had the measure of the Kangaroos.

Billy Boston scored his ninth Ashes try to beat Sully's short-lived record. In the last quarter of the match, Sully was denied a record equalling try; the referee ruled that he had not grounded the ball properly, which television afterwards showed was good. The referee's error was not crucial as the Lions won 17–10. Victory in the first two tests meant the Lions had once again retained the Ashes – a feat not achieved down under since 1928.

Sully was rested for the Sunday match when Wide Bay-Burnett were demolished 84–20 at Maryborough. He had a full week off before resuming on the left wing for a second meeting with NSW at the SCG the following Saturday. This time the match passed off without any unsavoury incidents; Sully scored a try as the Lions won 20–5.

After a gruelling match against NSW, there was no respite for Sully, who was included in the team to play Southern NSW at Wollongong the next day. Since retaining the Ashes, the Lions had relaxed their discipline, especially on Saturday nights. It was a rash thing to do before a match at Wollongong and the Lions paid the price, losing for a second time on tour, 18–10.

Once again, the test team was despatched to Coolangatta for special training. Having been readied for the fray, it was time for them to return to Sydney to take on the Australians at the SCG for the third and last time, on Saturday 14 July. There was just one change this time; Derek Turner was recalled at loose forward.

With Australian pride at stake, everyone expected a mighty contest. That's how it turned out with the Lions just about having the measure of the home side to reach half-time one point ahead. Then things turned sour. Sully, who was making his 15th consecutive appearance against the Kangaroos to equal Jim Sullivan's record, was sent off on 46 minutes by controversial local referee D'Arcy Lawler. Peter Dimond had broken through two tackles and looked certain to score when Sully came in off his wing and floored him with a bad high tackle. Sully was allegedly struck from behind by another Australian, who he assumed was his opposite number Ken Irvine. As Sully chased Irvine, Lawler immediately ordered him off. By the time the British reserves had left their seats in the stand to escort him to the dressing room, Sully had been involved in an altercation with a spectator. Two more players were ordered off – one from each side – as the Lions defended bravely before a late disputed try and conversion by Ken Irvine gave the Australians victory, 18–17, and prevented a first ever series whitewash.

Recalling the match nearly 50 years later for *No Sand Dunes in Featherstone*, Sully remembered that when the teams left the field his captain, an angry Eric Ashton, told him "You lost us that" and with it the chance to whitewash the Australians. In his defence, Sully told Ashton his dismissal was down to Lawler's bias and anyway "You didn't get any more (money) did you (for a whitewash)".

The Australian Board of Control judiciary committee held a meeting 30 minutes after the end of the test match. According to Phil King, when questioned by the judiciary committee, Sully "blew up". The committee did not appreciate Sully's attitude and as a result he was suspended for the rest of the Australian tour. The Australian Board of Control issued a statement: "The Board deplored Sullivan's demeanour at the inquiry and particularly his use of filthy language and uncomplimentary remarks to the Board and to the referee. These incidents will be reported by the Board to the team manager and to the

English League Council and a full transcript of the evidence will be sent to the English League Council." If the Board hoped to find sympathy for their actions they were disappointed; neither the team manager, a belligerent Stuart Hadfield, nor the RFL thought Sully had been wrong in his criticisms of that most partisan of referees, D'Arcy Lawler.

Having been suspended, Sully had to sit out the remainder of that section of the tour, missing the last two matches against the champions of the Sydney Premiership, St George, and Northern NSW.

Once the Australian leg of the tour was over, the injury-ridden party went onto New Zealand without their captain, Eric Ashton, and Don Fox. Soon after their arrival, Alex Murphy was also ruled out for the rest of the trip. Derek Turner took over as captain in Ashton's absence.

The first match was against Waikato at Huntly on Wednesday 25 July. Sully scored a try as the Lions won 59–20. After a satisfying opening victory, it was back to Auckland to prepare for the first test at Carlaw Park in three days time.

Due to the number of injuries, the tour managers had to select Sully at scrum half for the first test. For this match, Sully's usual left-wing spot was taken over by Wigan's Frank Carlton. It proved an unsuccessful switch and Sully swapped places with his half-back partner, Dave Bolton after 35 minutes. Their switch brought no marked improvement and the match ended with the Lions being nilled for the first time ever in a test against the Kiwis. The home side won 19–0.

After the first test, the tourists made their way south. Sully missed the matches against the Maoris at Wellington on Tuesday 31 July and Canterbury at Christchurch on Thursday 2 August.

Having easily accounted for Canterbury, Sully was recalled for a second match at the Show Grounds, against a New Zealand XIII on Saturday 4 August. He contributed two tries towards a 31–17 victory, achieved with only 12 men after Derek Turner was dismissed midway through the second half. For those chosen, there was the prospect of a gruelling 140 miles journey over the Southern Alps to Greymouth the following day. An early journey by rail and car, then the match and a late journey back was hardly enjoyable, but Sully managed to score a try in a 66–8 win over West Coast.

Two days later he was playing again, this time in Rotorua, one of the main centres of Maori Rugby League, against Bay of Plenty. Sully was replaced without scoring by Neil Fox during a match that saw the Lions' record their highest ever score, 81–14, in New Zealand.

Nursing a pulled muscle, Sully missed the test defeat against New Zealand at Carlaw Park on Saturday 11 August. Such was the toll of injuries that Peter Small of Castleford, normally a centre, had to make his test debut in place of Sully on the left wing. This was the first series defeat the Lions had suffered in New Zealand since 1950.

Sully was also ruled out of the final match in New Zealand, which saw the Lions' suffer their biggest ever defeat in New Zealand, 46–13, at the hands of Auckland, two days later. Altogether, Sully had made 18 appearances plus one as substitute in the 30 matches on the Australasian part of the tour scoring 14 tries. The prime objective of retaining the Ashes had been achieved, but injuries had hit the party hard and partially explain the six defeats – three in test matches – the Lions had suffered.

But this long tour was not over yet. Sully was a member of a squad of 17 players who were chosen to travel on to South Africa. Before setting off, Stuart Hadfield let Bill Fallowfield know that the players were exhausted, but the response from Leeds gave him no leeway – arrangements had been made and must be honoured. Having bade farewell to another six injured tourists who were heading for home, the remainder of the party departed Sydney on Saturday 18 August, flying onto Perth, had a refuelling stop on the Cocos Islands then a lay-over on Mauritius before landing in Johannesburg two days later.

One of the injured players to return home was Billy Boston, thus avoiding controversy – the strict apartheid laws in South Africa at this time would have made it very difficult for Boston to be part of the tour party for the matches in South Africa.

Despite the controversy over continuing the tour, the party was keen to make a good impression on the field, especially as the British Rugby Union team was just completing their own tour of the Republic. However, they faced a gruelling last leg, as over 10 days the tourists had to play two matches at altitude on the hard grounds of the High Veldt with a match in between at Durban where the weather on the shores of the Indian Ocean would be warm and humid.

Since being substituted at Rotorua, there had been two weeks of recovery time and Sully was fit to stake his claim for the left wing position in the matches scheduled against the Rugby League of South

Africa (RLSA), which had launched its first season with five clubs in mid-July. Although the RLSA had some former Springboks in its ranks, its players were nearly all newcomers to rugby league. Dave Brown, a leading Australian coach, had spent three months in the Republic working with the players, but his efforts could not make up for the lack of match experience. Without that, the RLSA teams had only a limited knowledge of defensive tactics and were no match for the tourists.

Two rival competitions had started in South Africa in 1962, and earlier in their season, Wakefield Trinity had been invited to tour by the National Rugby League. Even a combined side of the best players from both competitions would have struggled against the Lions.

The first match took place under floodlights at Pretoria on Thursday 23 August where the Lions won 49–30. The tourists then made the 330 mile journey from Pretoria to Durban by overnight train. Injuries were a major problem and the party's resources were stretched so thin that Colin Hutton, who had ended his playing career five years earlier, had to be pressed into service as a stand-in substitute and actually replaced Ike Southward during the match in Durban on the following Saturday. Hutton's on-field presence was certainly necessary as the RLSA XIII came close to springing a surprise. Sully scored two tries as the Lions just held on to win 39–33.

There was some time for site-seeing but the party was practically too drained to take the opportunity before the tour wound up with a third meeting with the RLSA under lights at the Rand Stadium in Johannesburg on the evening of Friday 31 August. Sully, one of 10 tourists who played in all three matches in the Republic, signed off in style, scoring a hat-trick of tries in a 45–23 win.

The matches were well received in South Africa, and were certainly better fare than the Lions and France had provided in 1957. In 1963, a united competition was played, and in July and August a South African rugby league team toured Australia and New Zealand. But after that the game collapsed, leaving players who had committed to play rugby league unable to return to the then strictly amateur rugby union code.

Then there was just time to pack before the 6,000 mile journey home. Sully arrived back in England, slightly later than expected due to flight delays, on the evening of Saturday 1 September. He was very pleased to be home and even happier some weeks later when the tour's record profits produced a player bonus was of £571/14/9 (£571.74).

110

14. A final season with Saints

The tour of South Africa meant Sully had missed the usual pre-season friendly against Liverpool City on 10 August and the first couple of weeks of the new fixture format for 1962–63. As part of the introduction of two divisions, the league programme was preceded by two new short competitions – the Eastern and Western Divisional Championships, combining First and Second Division clubs. To maintain local rivalries which had been disrupted by the introduction of two divisions, each league club had to play two others that were from the same region, but outside its own division.

While Sully was away in South Africa, St Helens had announced a couple of rugby union recruits. Both made scoring league debuts against Salford on 18 August and went on to have a major impact oat the club. The best known of the two names was the Welsh international full-back, Kel Coslett, but the other was a South African wingman, Len Killeen, who was a direct rival for Sully's left wing shirt.

At least, after such a long arduous tour, Sully did not announce his retirement as he had threatened. He needed some time to rest and unlike Dick Huddart, who rushed back into Saints colours at the first opportunity, Sully, like some other tourists, took a couple of weeks off. As he got ready to return to action, Ramon Joyce (Raymond Fletcher) was preparing an article for the October issue of *Tom Webb's Rugby League Record*. In the article, celebrating a vintage era for great wingers, Joyce placed Sully in the top four describing him as "the greatest English winger for a long, long time." His standing in the game seemed unassailable, but the season ahead would not be kind.

Sully finally returned to the Saints first team for the visit to Knotty Ash on Saturday 22 September. Playing right centre, he marked his return with a try in a 32–3 victory over Liverpool City in the Western Division competition. By then, the Saints board had given an even clearer indication that wholesale changes were in prospect by offloading both Ken Large and Austin Rhodes to Leigh.

Having delayed his return to action so long, Sully had already missed Yorkshire's winning start in the County Championship, which was played on Wednesday 19, and was overlooked for the second on 26 September. Although he had missed the first two rounds of the competition, Sully retained his place at right centre for St Helens'

Lancashire Cup semi-final at Oldham on Tuesday 2 October. A 10–8 victory at Watersheddings put the Saints in the final for the fifth consecutive year.

Seven wins and a draw had left St Helens in second place in the table at the end of the Western Division competition. Widnes, having finished third, had to visit Knowsley Road in the Divisional play-off semi-final. Saints' supporters had every right to hope their team might be the first to put its name on the new title, but Widnes got the better of them, 10–9, on Wednesday 9 October.

Len Killeen's tenure on the left wing finally ended in mid-October and Sully returned to his old position in time for the Lancashire Cup final. Swinton provided the opposition once more and the venue once again was Central Park on Saturday 27 October. Played in torrential rain and strong wind, the match was undoubtedly a game of two halves. Playing with the storm, a converted van Vollenhoven try after 11 minutes and a later penalty goal put the Saints 7–0 up at the interval. When the teams switched round, Swinton could only record two penalty goals, which meant that at the final whistle, the Saints had won 7–4, to retain the trophy for another year and provide Sully with a second Lancashire Cup winners' medal.

At the request of the FRL, the RFL's international committee agreed on Wednesday 29 August to an extended international programme this season. After being inactive for six years, the England team was resurrected for this season. So instead of appearing for the Saints at Castleford, Sully gained his third England cap against France at Headingley on Saturday 17 November. England won 18–6.

As they reflected on their defeat in the Eastern Division Final on 10 November, Huddersfield's directors looked for ways of strengthening their team. An experienced threequarter was seen as a pressing need and within days the Huddersfield board had made an approach to St Helens for Sully, offering £2,500. This offer was rejected by the Saints' board on 27 November, when it was agreed to accept no less than £4,500 for him.

Despite the uncertainty hanging over him, Sully was one of only five of the summer's Australasian tour party – the other four being Eric Ashton, Neil Fox, Laurie Gilfedder and Derek Turner – who were chosen to face France at Perpignan on Sunday 2 December. So while his Saints team mates made the long trek north to Workington, Sully was off to France on what was very much a trip into the unknown. Ten of the players had faced the France for England two weeks before. With seven players due to make their test debuts it was still a highly inexperienced team and it failed to deal with a biased local referee in a roughhouse. In such conditions Great Britain lost 17–12, a third consecutive defeat at the hands of the French.

As the season approached its mid-point, it seemed clear from the number of changes being made each week that Stan McCormick was still searching for his best back line up. Sully seemed to have accepted that Len Killeen's arrival had put his left wing spot in jeopardy, but he remained unsure about his own position in the team.

Three days after appearing in Perpignan, the Saints' board seem to have decided it was time to resolve the question of which position by letting Sully go; they put him on the transfer list at a fee of £6,000. He played in the 13–8 victory over Leeds on the following Saturday, 8 December, and was said by a number of reporters to have justified the fee placed on him. His old club, Huddersfield maintained its interest, and increased its offer to £3,500 at a meeting held with Saints' officials later that same evening. However, it was felt unlikely that Sully would agree to move back to Yorkshire and Saints at this stage wanted more money.

Talks between Sully and Saints chairman Harry Cook were held later in the month after the winger had missed Thursday evening training. Explaining his absence from training, Sully told a reporter: "On Thursday my job took me on a round trip of 250 miles in the Midlands. I had a breakdown, and when I got home late the ankle which I damaged at Leeds last Saturday was starting to feel sore again." Talks with Cook with following Tuesday made no progress, the Saints chairman said that Sully "would not listen".

In response Sully explained that he might as well carry out his earlier threat and retire. As he told reporters: "I don't really want to leave St Helens because they are a good club, but they mustn't really want me or they would have taken me off the list.

Since I joined St Helens, I don't think I have played five consecutive games in the same position. I am tired of being moved around. I prefer centre to wing these days but I don't like the idea of being picked on the right one week and on the left the next.

113

I just don't know where I am. Recently, for example Wilf Smith, who is a half-back, was brought into the team at centre. To accommodate him I was moved from right to left. Why was I the one to be switched? No player can give of his best under those conditions."

It was one thing agreeing to play anywhere when asked by Alan Prescott before he signed for St Helens, but this constant chopping and changing was not what he had expected.

In his column in the *Daily Express*, Jack Bentley reported on a conversation with Jean that highlighted the strains Mick's playing career imposed on their marriage: "I'll be quite honest. I don't want Mick to play again. I think he's had enough rugby – and I certainly have. It's been rugby, rugby, rugby for most of our married life and I reckon it's time football took a back seat.

Our six-year-old boy, David, has not seen much of his Dad over the past few years because of football. Mick has been to Australia three times since David was born, and I've been told David was fretting at school while Mick was away last summer."

In a bid to break the deadlock, Sully, who was out of work at the time, let it be known that he was prepared to move anywhere provided he could be found work and suitable accommodation. There were, however, rumours that South Sydney were prepared to pay the fee and recruit Sully as player-coach. Other rumours linked Sully to a New Zealand club.

This was the season of the big freeze; Boxing Day marked the start of the most severe winter weather of the 20th century. Heavy snow and gales marked the end of the old year before, as the country lay blanketed in snow and ice, the New Year began with the coldest January for nearly 150 years. Rivers and even parts of the sea froze. Freezing temperatures continued into February which brought further large falls of snow. Eventually, faced with a huge fixture backlog, the RFL agreed to extend the season until 1 June.

When the plummeting temperatures put the game into cold storage, Sully had made 12 appearances for Saints – six at right centre, three at left centre and three on the left wing. He had scored just one try. Although his form was not good, Sully still had his admirers and it was thought that Leeds might come in with a bid. Huddersfield's board was still keen and made a second attempt to sign him just hours before the Challenge Cup deadline. This time Saints agreed to accept £2,000,

£1,000 less than they had rejected a few weeks earlier, but Sully refused to move. Sully, who had not been seen at Knowsley Road since he was transfer-listed, gave no indication of his future plans.

At the start of February, Sully returned to training and asked that he be given a settled position to prove his ability. With pitches ice bound, the players had to try and keep in shape by training in a school gym, supplemented by sessions on the running track under the stand at Knowsley Road.

The chance came when, finally, in early March a thaw started and soon the snow and ice was gone. The thaw that made the pitches playable once more also seemed to warm up relations around Knowsley Road. Having had time to consider his options Sully decided that the time was not right to retire. He reported again for training and the Saints board welcomed him back.

St Helens had been out of action from the home win over Hull on 22 December until they travelled over to play Hull KR on Saturday 9 March. That was the first time the whole fixture list had gone ahead this year. Sully was back in the team which lost to the Robins 3–2.

Two days later, the first round of the Challenge Cup, delayed a month, took Saints over to Thrum Hall where they lost 9–2. A further two-week break seems to have rejuvenated Sully who scored a hat-trick when Bramley visited St Helens on Saturday 23 March.

There were some major disappointments for Sully as this extraordinary season regained momentum. When the RFL selection committee met on Monday 20 March it made wholesale changes to December's test team. Although Sully had played on the Saturday at Bramley, there was no place for him in either the team or the shadow team for the test match against France to be played at Wigan on Wednesday 3 April. It appeared to be a clear signal that Sully's test days were over.

Also, back in the autumn, Clive Churchill on behalf of South Sydney, Sully's favourite club in Sydney, had made him an offer to play the close season in Australia. No one had taken a short-term contract before and Sully was keen to accept the offer. St Helens gave permission in mid-November provided that three conditions were met: that the RL Council approved the move, that the Australian club he would be joining deposited £10,000 in an English bank as security and that he was back in time for the start of the next season. Sully was said to have been offered £1,000 plus match pay and a good job for his stint down under. All he needed was official approval, but at the RL Council meeting, held on Monday 8 April, Sully was refused permission to play for an Australian club over the summer, apparently by one vote.

The movement of players between England and Australia had always been a difficult one for the game. Both countries recognised that international players were an attraction, but also were concerned about weakening their own competition. For long periods in its history, there were international transfer bans, and the Council members were probably concerned that their own clubs could lose players who experienced and enjoyed a short time playing in Australia, and would want a permanent move; or would be injured and unable to start the following season with their English clubs.

Clearing the fixture backlog meant there was a hectic run in to the end of the season. St Helens, like every other club, had to play twice a week for two months. St Helens' challenge for the Championship faltered in April when they lost to an in-form Swinton away on Easter Saturday and at home two days later in front of a 19,100 crowd. Sully missed only one match in those two months, at the Boulevard on 27 April, which ended in another defeat. Two days later, Wakefield Trinity inflicted a fourth defeat on Saints at Knowsley Road. Saints got back to winning ways, but the title had slipped away. Swinton, who never faltered, went on to finish top, six points ahead of Saints who took the runners up position on points average over Widnes.

Sully's form if not his fortunes appeared to have taken a turn for the better and he ended the season strongly, running in eight tries in his last 15 appearances. However, unbeknown to the fans, Sully had made his last appearance and scored his last try for Saints in their last league fixture of the season, a 24–9 defeat of Oldham at Watersheddings on 30 May. He signed off on an unsettled season which had produced just 14 tries from his 31 matches.

116

15. York

Fortunately, with a lucrative summer 'down under' no longer a possibility, Sully obtained some temporary work over the close season with the possibility that this could be made permanent. However, times were hard and he unsuccessfully applied to the Saints' board for a loan of £150 in June.

Amidst all this uncertainty there was a new addition to the family, Michelle was born on 18 July 1963. Around that time a move to Barrow as player-coach looked possible, provided the 'Shipbuilders' would meet at least £2,000 of the asking price of £3,000. That move also faltered and Sully seemed destined to return to Knowsley Road for pre-season training at the start of August.

By then, the atmosphere at Knowsley Road was growing tense. With attendances continuing to decline, the NRL management committee had taken action in June after consulting with the clubs. To try and reduce the possibility of clubs falling into financial difficulties, the management committee had instructed its members to amend their player terms; bonuses for league matches would no longer be allowed and winning pay must be no greater than twice losing pay.

Like a few other top clubs, St Helens offered their players amended terms of £20 for a win and £16 for a defeat away and £16 a win and £8 a defeat at home. This was not acceptable to many players, especially as the away terms were said to be worse than those of three years earlier. Saints' players along with those at Wakefield Trinity, Widnes and Wigan refused to re-sign for the coming season, which threw the opening day fixtures into doubt. As the management committee made threats about possible repercussions, a meeting of players and officials from the four clubs was arranged for Knowsley Road on Friday 16 August. However, before he could have his say at that meeting, a new opportunity had presented itself and Sully needed to be elsewhere. His time at St Helens was over. He had made 82 appearances for the club and scored 31 tries for 93 points while at Knowsley Road.

Although still on the right side of 30, Sully surprisingly agreed to a transfer to York, for around £2,000, on that Friday. His contract with York stipulated he must live in the city, so Mick and Jean went house hunting the following day, when he probably had been expecting to play for Saints in the usual charity opener against Liverpool City.

A halt was soon called to house hunting, as Mick and Jean decided to embark on a new venture as landlord and landlady of the Royal Oak on Goodramgate, a busy pub in the heart of the city.

York, where his old Test team mate Tommy Harris was the coach, had finished third in the first season of Second Division rugby and were obviously hoping that Sully's experience would strengthen their drive for one of the two promotion places. His signing certainly raised expectations amongst the club's fans of better times ahead.

One week after signing, Sully made his debut for York in the opening league match at the Willows on 24 August against a struggling Salford side. Two tries on his debut was in many ways a dream start, but York, with only 11 men for most of the second half lost 23–21.

Sully's move back over the Pennines meant that this season he would be playing in the Eastern Division. To try and increase interest, the Divisional Championship's fixtures had been spread throughout the season. York's opening fixture was against First Division Hull at Wiggington Road on 11 September. Sully was moved over to left centre for this match which York won 17–7.

Sully's decision to drop into the Second Division appeared to confirm to the selectors that he had turned his back on top flight rugby. Certainly the Yorkshire selectors seem to have seen it that way and he was not chosen for either match in the County Championship or for the match against the touring Australians.

More likely, he was overlooked because of York's slow start in the league and departure from the Yorkshire Cup in the first round at lowly Doncaster. Although many journalists said that playing in the Second Division was a block to higher honours, that certainly did not appear to be the case. Sully's successor in both the Yorkshire and Great Britain teams this season was Norman Field who was playing for Second Division Batley.

Sully was not one of only five 1962 tourists – Eric Ashton, Dave Bolton, Neil Fox, Vince Karalius and Alex Murphy – chosen for the first test, which was held for the first time under lights at Wembley. Sully's reign on Great Britain's left wing against Australia which had lasted since 1954 was over. As holders of both the Ashes and the World Cup, Great Britain went into the series as favourites. But, it was undoubtedly a mistake to field a new look Great Britain team, with an experimental pack containing three new caps, to take on an Australian outfit who

118

would be fiercely competitive even if their strength had not been obviously clear so far.

From the start at Wembley it was a physical contest and Alex Murphy suffered a broken nose on 14 minutes, but played on. When Great Britain, trailing 2–0, lost stand-off Dave Bolton with a dislocated shoulder, Eric Ashton moved to stand-off and Ken Bowman moved out of the pack in to the centres. Playing a man short for nearly an hour, Great Britain could not hold the Australian pack and suffered a record home defeat.

In the wake of a depleted Great Britain's defeat in the first test, the selectors met on Monday 28 October and considered what changes to make. Injury had ruled out Dave Bolton and he was replaced by Frank Myler of Widnes. Having bravely gone for experimentation the selectors decided to err on the side of experience and recalled four of the 1962 tourists – three forwards, Brian Edgar, Dick Huddart and Derek Turner, and Sully. Before the match all three of those great forwards withdrew which left the team with a different but equally experimental look.

Sully had been recalled to make his first ever test appearance on the right wing. So far for York, Sully had made five appearances at right centre and four at left centre, so it is understandable that for Alfred Drewry, Sully's selection was a confession of weakness which could not "be read as other than a defensive move". There was a lot depending on the second test at Swinton and the preparation before it, and so instead of preparing for a Second Division clash at the Watersheddings, Sully was on his way to meet up with his test team mates at Wilderspool on Thursday 7 November.

Sully was only the sixth York player to be selected for Great Britain, although his team-mate, Geoff Smith, became the seventh three weeks later when he was also selected to face the Australians when he replaced Sully.

A 30,843 crowd in the ground and a large television audience were expecting a hard fought battle and briefly it appeared that Great Britain might get the better of it when Swinton's John Stopford, playing on the left wing, raced in for a try after 10 minutes. That was before serious rib injuries to Frank Myler, who was forced to retire after 20 minutes, and Eric Ashton, who struggled on to half-time, reduced the effectiveness of the Lions team. Superb Australian backing up ruthlessly exploited the Lions' defensive frailty to run in seven tries before half-time for a 31–8 lead.

After the break, the 11-man British team tried hard, but the Kangaroos maintained the pressure and scored another five tries to set up a new record score, 50–12. It was also the highest winning margin ever recorded in an Ashes test. Such a resounding defeat dealt a massive blow to British pride and meant the loss of the Ashes at home for the first time since 1911–12.

In the aftermath of that very unhappy return to the test arena, Sully was one of seven members of the British team that day who would never again pull on a Lions' jersey. It was a sad end to what had been a glittering test career. Desperate to restore some pride in the third Test, the selectors rang the changes once again, bringing in another six new caps. Only one of those new caps was a Second Division player, Geoff Smith, Sully's sometime right wing partner at York.

Life in the NRL was also proving somewhat traumatic. The fixture planners had not scheduled any meetings with Bradford Northern in the Eastern Division and arranged the two Second Division fixtures in the second half of the season; at York on 18 January with the return at Odsal Stadium set for Easter Tuesday, 31 March. Four weeks before their first meeting, Northern's board announced that the club, which was bottom of Division Two, was effectively bankrupt and unable to fulfil its fixtures. The results of what fixtures Northern had completed were eventually expunged from the NRL and Eastern Division tables.

In the aftermath of Bradford Northern's dramatic collapse, the NRL's membership was forced to reconsider its options. An EGM was held, on 16 February, almost exactly halfway through the two-division scheme's three season trial. York was one of the supporters of a proposal to stay with two divisions, but with the added incentive of four up and four down, but that was defeated by 21 votes to 6. Instead a second proposal, to revert to a single division for 1964–65, was carried by 23 votes to 4. At a stroke the need to drive for a promotion place was removed.

There were brief hopes at Wiggington Road of a Challenge Cup run after a home victory over Bramley on 8 February, but they were ended by a visit from the eventual finalists, Hull KR, on the final day of that month.

Sully playing for York. (Photo: Courtesy *Rugby League Journal*)

Sully was missing from the team for the whole of March and the early part of April. One of the matches he missed, at Rochdale, was played under an experimental play-the-ball rule – the ball could be played anyway but backwards – at the start of April. The experiment should have continued through until the end of the season, but when Sully returned to play in the last three matches the new rule, having been so derided, had been scrapped after just one weekend.

It had turned out to be a very disappointing season for York. In the Eastern Division Championship, York's final match, against Featherstone Rovers in mid-April, ended in a draw, providing the club's first point since the opening match against Hull. That left the 'Minstermen' in 13th place in the Eastern Division table. There was just time for two final league matches, one won and one lost, which meant they finally finished seventh in the Second Division. Over his first season at York, Sully had made 21 appearances, scoring seven tries.

1964–65

Over the summer, York's financial problems had caused disquiet in the squad, especially among the forwards. Dennis Goodwin, Sully's fellow tourist in 1958 announced his retirement, while others, such as Albert Firth and Dave Lamming, wanted to move away from the club. With few adequate recruits in prospect, the promise shown by the club a year earlier had dimmed.

Sully's playing career with York lasted just four more matches. His final appearance for the 'Wasps' came in a 23–12 defeat at Rochdale on Tuesday 1 September. In his time with York this season, there was just one win, over Dewsbury, during which Sully was sent off midway through the second half. By the time he had served his two match suspension, Sully had completely lost interest and let the York board know, in mid-September, that he would be taking a job in St Helens and would be leaving the city in due course. Effectively he had crossed himself off York's register. In total, Sully had made 28 appearances for York scoring six tries.

It was not just the rugby that had lost its attraction. York had never really felt like home, so a move away sounded like a good idea. When the job in St Helens fell through the family packed up and moved to Dewsbury to be nearer Jean's parents.

16. Dewsbury and Junee

The family settled down in Dewsbury. Sully, who was aged 30, got a job at the gasworks and Jean later opened a hairdressing salon near the town centre.

After a few months inactivity, the *Rugby Leaguer* reported that Sully was going to get involved with the Dewsbury Celtic amateur club. It even went as far as saying that Celtic had approached York to ask for Sully's services as a coach and player on permit. York agreed and it looked likely that Sully was about to begin a new life in the amateur game. However, Sam Morton, who was one of Celtic's leading players at the time, has no recollection of him ever coming along to training and he certainly never appeared for the club.

If that was the plan, then it was derailed by an approach to Sully by two Dewsbury directors – Les Driver and Donald Green – who wanted to bring his experience to their club. Sully was interested and York did not prove to be a stumbling block. They readily agreed to him joining Dewsbury on loan until the end of the season. Having received a small down-payment and agreed his match terms, Sully raised his fitness levels and was ready to make his debut at Halifax on Saturday 20 March.

1965 Dewsbury team. Back: Mick Sullivan, Taylor, Lowe, Naylor, Walker, Mullins, Newall; front: Hirst, Rawes, Firth, Osborne, Marsh, Bates.
(Photo: Courtesy Robert Gate)

That plan was spoilt by a heavy fall of snow which caused the match to be postponed. It was re-arranged for the following Wednesday, but a flooded pitch caused a further postponement. Finally Sully was able to make his debut in a 2–2 draw at Bramley a week later than planned.

He had joined a club whose standing was about on a par with York; neither club was particularly successful at that time. Sully had been brought into a reshuffled threequarter line on the right wing and played in the last nine league matches of the season there, scoring one try.

Dewsbury finished in 21st place, eight points below Barrow who claimed the 16th spot and entry into the League's Championship play-offs, which had been extended to include the top–16 clubs this season in an attempt to sustain interest in the competition.

Without Sully's assistance, Dewsbury Celtic had enjoyed a very successful season. They had qualified for the first round of the Challenge Cup, won the Yorkshire Junior Cup and led the Leeds and District League. At Celtic's end of season function, Sully was the guest of honour and presented a trophy to each member of the team.

Sully's move to Dewsbury was made permanent for the 1965–66 season, but the team did not get off to the best possible start. Having played in the opening match, a defeat at Salford, Sully missed the next two defeats as well as the welcome first win of the season over Bramley at Crown Flatt. He was back in the team, on the right wing, for the first round of the Yorkshire Cup at home on Sunday 4 September. Dewsbury took an early lead, but Huddersfield had other ideas and quickly squashed any home hopes of a Cup run and won 27–4.

Fearing a mediocre season was on the cards, Dewsbury's directors decided to sack their coach, Charlie Seeling junior, in mid-September. Alvyn Newall took over in the interim while the board reviewed a shortlist that included Laurie Gant, Jim Ledgard, Allen Lockwood, Les Pearce and Mick Sullivan. It was not unanimous, but Sully received the support of the majority of the committee and was appointed as Dewsbury's captain-coach. Joining Dewsbury had revived Sully's love of the game and in turn his drive and enthusiasm revived the old club. Sully set about refashioning the talented squad he inherited into a team in his own boisterous, combative image.

124

Sully and Alex Murphy lead out their teams before the Dewsbury versus
St Helens Challenge Cup semi-final. (Photo: Courtesy Alex Service)

Freezing weather caused a few postponements at the start of 1966, the
last for Dewsbury was the visit of Widnes on Saturday 19 February.
After that the weather relented and the Challenge Cup campaign was
able to get underway as scheduled the following Saturday.

With his weight up to almost 15 stones, Sully decided early in the
New Year to take over as loose-forward. Relishing his move into the
pack, Sully led an unsung Dewsbury side which generally contained
another seven or eight Shaw Cross products on an unexpected run in
the Challenge Cup, made all the sweeter because Sully reckoned he
had put a £2 bet on the club to lift the trophy which would have
brought him a £1,000 windfall.

Dewsbury's first tie was at Lawkholme Lane, where they secured
their first away win of the season, beating Keighley 5–4. The next
round on Saturday 19 March brought Barrow to Crown Flatt. Sully's
team did just enough to beat Barrow, 23–15.

125

The quarter-final draw gave Dewsbury another home tie, against Huddersfield. This should have been played on Saturday 2 April, but heavy snowfalls across the north of England caused all the ties to be postponed. Dewsbury rescheduled for the afternoon of Tuesday 5 April and were rewarded with a 9,300 crowd at Crown Flatt. Sully had managed to dispel any memories of the earlier Yorkshire Cup defeat from his players' minds and an early try by Alvyn Newall gave Dewsbury the edge. They won a hard forward battle, 8–2.

The draw for the Challenge Cup semi-final set up a meeting with a strong St Helens team, led by Alex Murphy, at Swinton on Saturday 16 April. Dewsbury's first peacetime semi-final appearance for 37 years turned into a titanic struggle. With Wembley Stadium only 80 minutes away, Dewsbury's team certainly did not lack for motivation. Facing a Saints team who were probably over confident, Dewsbury took full advantage. They took an early 5–0 lead through an Alvyn Newall drop-goal and Geoff Marsh try. Having gone ahead, they defended doggedly, came up quickly to swamp the first receiver and killed any ball movement. Despite losing stand-off Alan Edwards with a broken jaw, Dewsbury still led on the hour, before two Len Killeen tries saved Saints' day.

Before the final whistle confirmed St Helens as the winners, 12–5, and that his bet was lost, Sully flew in to tackle Ray French who was running the ball out from his own line. Sully's head accidentally made contact with French's knee and he had to be carried off unconscious. He was still in a semi-conscious state when he was driven home. Dewsbury's chance of glory was over, but Sully remained convinced that part of the reason for the defeat lay with the referee, Eric Clay, who had been, in his mind, unduly influenced by Alex Murphy into allowing Saints to get away with head-high tackles while penalising his own team for the same offence.

Ray French recalled this tackle in his book on 100 *Great Rugby League Players*. He said that Sully's "... raw courage and defiance, his astute rugby brain and ferocious tackling in that match were still instinctive to him, although he was at the end of a great career."

Sully's concussion was severe enough to rule him out of the remaining two weeks and six matches of the season. In his absence, Dewsbury finished in a very disappointing 24th place.

Junee

After the Cup semi-final, Sully had been contacted by Eddie Waring with an offer of a contract to play and coach in Australia for the summer. Waring warned Sully that the contract might have some issues attached, but the offer was a good one and it was very tempting. The contract was being offered by Junee, a junior club in the Riverina region of southern NSW, nearly 300 miles west of Sydney. And it was a good offer – his return air fare costing $1,200, $2,000 for the season plus a job and $50 per week. (At the time an Australian dollar = £0.39) It was not an easy decision to make because Jean was pregnant, but in the end – with Dewsbury's approval – Sully accepted and agreed to leave for Australia immediately the British season ended.

Junior clubs in Riverina had tried to sign a number of big-name players, mostly Kiwis, over their close season, but Sully was the only one to sign on the dotted line. Part of the reason for that lack of success was that the issues Sully had been warned about were major ones. Junee was one of eight clubs, the so called 'Riverina Rebels', who had formed the Murrumbidgee Rugby League, and were in the process of breaking away from the NSW Country RL over boundary disputes. Once the rebels had walked out they were immediately blacklisted by the Australian Board of Control.

Such was his fame that Sully was the centre of attention when he arrived in Sydney at the end of April. A press conference was organised at the airport where Sully took a bullish stance. He told waiting television reporters and newspapermen that he had taken legal advice and even though Junee was now out of bounds he did not fear suspension. The press conference went on for so long that Sully missed his intended connecting flight to Wagga Wagga.

In reality, having signed the contract, used the air ticket and needing the money to support Jean and his family back in Britain, Sully probably had no choice but to play. For joining the rebel competition, he was suspended sine die by the RFL in June, officially for playing there without clearance. Sully had played eight matches for Junee when he received word from Dewsbury that Jean's pregnancy was not going well and that he should return home immediately. He packed and left Australia in mid-July.

Pre-season training for the 1966–67 season was underway when Sully got back to England. Brearley Bailey, the Dewsbury chairman, told reporters that Sully was expected at Crown Flatt on Friday 22 July when he would "inform the committee of any steps he had in mind regarding his future and of any appeal to the NRL". What they heard was that Sully was keen to resume his coaching duties as soon as possible and that he would be lodging an appeal against his suspension right away.

It might have been expected that this would not be straightforward, but on hearing Sully's explanation the RFL surprisingly agreed at its meeting on 24 August to reinstate him while issuing a reprimand for a technical breach of the rules. This decision allowed Sully to take over as Dewsbury's player-coach for the start of the season.

It was a cause of friction that Sully did not have the final say in Dewsbury's team selection. He would pick a team for each match, but the club's selection committee had final approval and generally made some changes. After reacting badly to being baited by a disgruntled fan over the quality of 'his' teams, Sully was called before the club committee. With only a draw and three defeats to show so far, the outcome was inevitable. Sully was sacked.

Only one good thing came out of being sacked. Dewsbury did as he asked and crossed him off the playing register. Sully had played his final match for Dewsbury, a replayed Yorkshire Cup tie, at Wakefield on Monday 5 September. Following that defeat he became a free agent, having made 40 appearances for the club.

There were more pressing issues to be addressed. On Tuesday 6 September Mick and Jean's second son, John, was born prematurely. It was three months before Mick and Jean were allowed to take John home. As they paid daily visits to the hospital, the issue of Sully's suspension rumbled on. Following protests about the lifting of the earlier suspension, the Australian Rugby League was informed by the RFL in October that Sully was no longer on the Dewsbury or any other club's register.

As he looked for ways to strengthen his team, which seemed unable to stem a long losing streak, Doncaster's coach, Les Belshaw, approached Sully. A deal was struck and Belshaw tried to add him to his squad at the end of November. This proved problematic when Sully's registration was put before the NRL management committee on

14 December. After due consideration, the management committee refused the request. Clearly he was frozen out of the game. Disappointed, Sully announced that he would be returning to Australia to coach and this time he would take his whole family with him.

His mind made up, the whole family emigrated under the assisted passage scheme for the bargain price of £20. Sully was back in Junee in time to take charge ahead of the regular season which resumed in April 1967.

While playing in a pre-season friendly at Wagga Wagga, Sully suffered the most serious injury of his career. His jaw was broken in seven places when an opponent fell on him. He was put out of action for eight weeks and lost four stones before he could eat properly again.

In July 1968, Sully was released from the remainder of his contract by Junee and he and Jean considered what to do next. Under the terms of the assisted passage scheme, migrants had to repay their outward fares if they returned home within two years. When that point had been passed they had a major decision to make.

Another contract in Australia was a possibility and David, then aged 12, was keen to stay and develop his promising start in rugby league. However, Jean was keen to return to England and that in the end was what they did. It was a decision they both came to regret. But before that, they took the chance to travel home in some style on a P&O liner. As the Sullivans made their decision to leave, the Murrumbidgee League finally settled its differences with the Australian Board of Control and its member clubs were reinstated at the start of 1969.

Left: At work in Australia. Right: Mick with John and Michelle in Australia

David, Jean, John and Michelle just before leaving Australia.

17. Coaching and beyond

As he prepared to return to England in summer 1969, Sully was anticipating to apply to become Derek Turner's successor as coach at Castleford, but he arrived back in the country one day too late. The job at Wheldon Road went instead to his old Huddersfield team-mate, Tommy Smales.

Sully found a job as a pipe fitter on the construction of a new power station at Fiddlers Ferry near Warrington. While his family settled in to a house at Shaw Cross, Sully took lodgings near the construction site.

After contemplating working with Jack Broome at Huyton, Sully eventually resumed training at Leigh where Alex Murphy was captain-coach in October. His fitness returning, Sully thought he might be able to play in the second-row. Leigh's management were interested, and believed that Sully could operate as play-maker in the pack in support of Murphy.

On the verge of returning to action, Sully travelled over with Leigh to Batley on Sunday 19 October. Although not playing, it turned out to be a good day for Sully who won a new Ford Escort car in the half-time draw. He was a worthy winner as a report from him about the Junee 200 club, contained in a letter to Les Driver who was now on the Batley board, had inspired the club's draw.

That same day, he also let Leigh know that he had been offered the chance to coach and therefore his comeback plans were cancelled. A vacancy had arisen at Bradford Northern where Albert Fearnley had relinquished his coaching responsibilities once he had taken over the secretary's duties. Sully had accepted the job at Odsal, for which he would receive a wage plus travelling expenses, and would be starting immediately.

Sully inherited an experienced squad, but there were obviously some problems because Northern were slipping down the table. Sully set to work, but when he received his first payments he questioned the amount. He was told that his expenses for training and match preparation at Odsal were being paid on the basis of him travelling from Dewsbury, not from Widnes where he was still working. When the club would not reconsider its stance Sully resigned after just six weeks.

In the summer of 1970, Dave Cox, Batley's coach-manager for the previous two-and-a-half years, had moved to Australia and Sully was asked by the board to step in at the start of the new season. In the old style single division there were only limited opportunities for a small club like Batley to chase, but Sully's biggest obstacles were off the field rather than on. Those obstacles were to be found within the committee room and centred on team selection. In such situations the committee always held the upper hand and inevitably Sully was sacked after only a few weeks. Batley's committee promoted the long-serving 'A' team coach, John Westbury, to fill the vacancy.

Not long afterwards Sully came in for a lot of criticism when he stirred up a controversy after selling his story to *The People* newspaper. The story, which was sensationalised for publication in December 1970, threatened to 'lift the lid' off the shadier aspects of the game. Labelled the 'Hatchet Man', Sully's revelations mainly concerned how he had stiff-armed opponents and the lack of professionalism in club administration. It was a sad series of articles that left a sour taste. In his defence, Sully said he needed the money, but some thought he was shunned afterwards because of some of the material that was published.

After losing his job as a pipe-fitter, Sully joined the prison service as a plumber in 1972, and became an officer at Wakefield Prison. Having lost contact, Norman Wainwright, by now also a member of the prison service, arranged to meet up with Sully again in the early 1970s and was surprised by how much he had changed, hardly recognising his old friend went he went into the staff club at Wakefield. The punishment Sully had taken on the field had taken its toll on his body and his hair had thinned.

In the end it was a bad knee, a direct result of all the wear and tear inflicted on it during his playing days that forced Sully to retire from the prison service in 1989. That was to be Sully's last paid employment. Soon afterwards, Jean closed down her hairdressing salon and joined him in retirement.

Although he took no further active part in the game he would always attend and regularly speak at the annual sportsman's dinners at Shaw Cross until his illness became too severe. He was a keen member of the Lions Association and always enjoyed attending their dinners. When the Rugby League Heritage Centre opened in Huddersfield he was appointed as a curator and took every opportunity to spend time and socialise over there.

When Dewsbury's new stadium on Owl Lane was completed, Sully was invited to perform the ceremonial kick-off to get the first match underway in September 1994. Once open, Sully, who had been made an honorary member, was able to enjoy spending time there watching the Rams' home matches.

While not directly involved, Sully still had his records. It took 30 years before someone finally managed to equal Sully's remarkable record of 46 test caps. That someone was Garry Schofield and he reached that mark when he came on in the third test against the touring Kangaroos at Elland Road in Leeds, on 20 November 1994. Schofield's achievement merited a special award – a glass rugby ball – which was later presented to him by Sully.

To recognise the contribution of the game's greatest players, the RFL launched the Hall of Fame with nine founder members in October 1988. Additional members were inducted over the next decade-and-a-half. In late 2007, a group of people got together to press for Great Britain's record cap holder, Mick Sullivan, to be honoured with a place in the Hall of Fame. Despite a groundswell of support for Sully to be inducted, no nominations were put forward as the RFL allowed the Hall of Fame to slip into a period of inactivity,

That inactivity coincided with the cruellest year, 2008. At the start of July, after a short illness, Jean passed away, delivering a blow to Sully from which he could never recover. It soon became clear from Sully's fading memory and his inability to recognise former teammates and friends that his health was in serious decline. At the start of the following January it became clear why when Sully was diagnosed with Alzheimer's. Very soon his illness had become so severe that he could no longer live on his own. His home for nearly 40 years had to be sold to pay for care and he eventually had to move into a nursing home.

Sully's illness did not mean he was forgotten by the game. In October 2009, the Rugby League Heritage Centre honoured Sully by inducting him as its third Legend. A celebration lunch was organised at the George Hotel by the Centre's curator Sam Morton. Over 100 guests, including civic dignitaries, family, friends and many former team mates attended to hear speakers including Johnny Whiteley, Mick Stephenson, Councillor Julie Stewart Turner, the Mayor of Kirklees, and Umesh

Ummatt, the managing director of the George Hotel, describe Sully's contribution to rugby league and his standing as the joint holder of the record number of test caps. To make the evening even more special there were greetings from down under, including a video message from his old adversary Peter Dimond.

Finally, after eight years inactivity, the RFL decided to revitalise the Hall of Fame in 2013. It was a timely restart for Sully who was inducted along with Lewis Jones, Martin Offiah and Garry Schofield. The induction took place at the World Cup Celebration Dinner held at Huddersfield on the evening of Friday 1 November, ahead of the England versus Ireland match the following day. Joining the Hall of Fame was an honour that, as Nigel Wood, the chief executive of the RFL said, recognised Mick Sullivan as one "of the greatest British sportsmen of the last century".

In 2009 Mick was inducted into the Rugby League Heritage Centre Legends. Guests with Mick in this picture include Peter Fox, Neil Fox, Johnny Whitely and Colin Hutton. (Photo: Sam Morton)

The Mayor of Kirklees, Councillor Julie Stewart Turner, and the then owner of The George Hotel, Umesh Ummatt and Mick with the display about him. (Photo: Sam Morton)

Mick and Jean with their two of their grandchildren, Scott and Aimee.

Michelle with Mick and Jean on her Wedding Day, 14 May 1983.

Family group at John's Wedding in 2015. From left Mia Sullivan, Michelle Sullivan, John Sullivan, Tracy Sullivan, Mick Sullivan, Sam Sullivan, Scott Sullivan, Aimee Sullivan, David Bullock.
(Photo: Ozzie Malik, Di Vinci Photography)

John, Michelle and David in 1989.

Left: Mick andhis grandaughter Aimee in 2013.

Middle: Father's Day 2015 with Michelle and Mia.

Bottom: Mick with his grandson Scott in 2013 at Scott's Wedding.

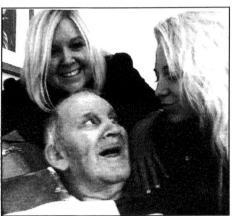

18. Memories of Mick Sullivan

Douglas Hird

I will never forget the day when young Mick Sullivan joined Shaw Cross Boys Club in the late 1940s. He came with his pal David Smith, the son of the late Harry V. Smith who was the secretary of the Dewsbury and Batley Amateur Rugby League.

They both became accomplished young rugby players. Mick was only a very slim lad when he set out to play the hard game of rugby league football, but he soon excelled. He was a talented youngster and he had the heart of a lion. He was competitive at everything he did. He did not just compete at rugby but also represented the club in athletics and swimming. He won the 100 yards and 220 yards races in the local athletics and then in the county athletic championships of the Yorkshire Association of Boys Clubs. He had pace; he was fast and showed great determination and Yorkshire grit in all the competitions he entered.

Mick and Norman Wainwright, another of his rugby pals, were both selected to represent England and played in the Under-18s in two international rugby union matches for the National Association of Boys' Clubs against Wales.

On the rugby field Mick had a tremendous sidestep and few could emulate him with such speed. He also became a formidable tackler and had no fear against the biggest opponent. It was obvious Mick was destined for the professional game and his remarkable success is well documented. Many thousands of boys have gone through the Shaw Cross Boys Club over the last 60 odd years and Mick Sullivan emerges as the greatest in my book.

Douglas Hird is the secretary of Shaw Cross Sharks ARLFC, a club he has served since the 1940s.

Norman Wainwright

I was 17 and Michael 16 when Stan Waring, club leader of Shaw Cross Boys' Club, introduced us. We became the best of friends and now we are octogenarians. I am pleased to say we still are.

The 'Pudsey Flier'; 11 stone wet through, tough, very strong and such an elusive runner. For me, he became a world class three quarter, not just a left wing man. His first appearance at left centre for Great Britain, speaks volumes of his ability. He learnt the game on the right wing. There's a difference between good and great, Michael was great. My best mate and plenty of laughs along the way.

After his marriage to Jean, he'd call for me on Sunday mornings. My mother would cook him a full English breakfast, then off to Tingley nine hole miniature golf for a game. These were good times. Happy memories of our friendship on and off the field. A good pal we were very close – like brothers. I am so proud of what he did for Rugby League.

Mrs and Mrs Sullivan, his parents, never called him by his nick name 'Mick'. I call him Michael in respect to their wishes. A nice chap from a nice family. A pleasure to have met them all.

Norman Wainwright played rugby league with Mick Sullivan at Shaw Cross Boys Club, and for the NABC England rugby union team. He also played professionally for Huddersfield and Batley.

Sam Morton

Mick Sullivan – Top rugby league man

Having known Mick for more than 50 years I would like to pay tribute to him as a top rugby league player and also a really modest man who was always willing to spend time to chat about rugby league and have a good laugh about life in general. Mick was a rugby league supporters man and was very easy to like.

On my first trip to Wembley for the final in 1958 when Wigan beat Workington Town and left-winger Mick scored a try, I admired the speed, skills, tackling and toughness that Mick displayed for his winning team, Wigan. It was just the same in 1959 and 1961 when Mick played in two more top Wembley Finals for Wigan and St Helens – three Finals and three winner's medals plus a Championship winner's medal and Lions tour test matches in Australia and New Zealand.

In Dewsbury town centre the Market House was a rugby league man's pub where over the years people could chat to Joe Lyman, Dewsbury's captain in the first Wembley Final in 1929 when they played Wigan. Mick was a visitor to the pub, as was Arthur Keegan who played full-back for Hull FC against Mick in the 1959 Wembley Final and was a Great Britain Lions tourist in 1966. What a thrill it was to meet and chat to these rugby league legends along with many other rugby league players who called in for a pint. Happy days.

From 2005 to 2011 I was the curator of Stevo's Rugby League Heritage Centre / Museum at The George Hotel in Huddersfield. Mick Sullivan was the first player to be inducted into The Rugby League Heritage Centre Legends. Mick's family plus 100 guests were thrilled to see him receive the accolade he deserved and the George Hotel owners and staff always gave him respect for his achievements in rugby league. Over the years at the Museum many visitors from Australia who stayed at the Hotel were always asking about Mick Sullivan. On several occasions I took Mick from Dewsbury to The George Hotel for him to meet his many overseas fans from the 1950s and 60s. Very happy days for everyone concerned. One lovely comment from an Australian rugby league man was "The only thing wrong with Mick Sully is that he is 'A Pom'. He should have been an Aussie, but he is still my hero."

Sully also played in three World Cup competitions and five Ashes series. He wore the Great Britain shirt on almost 80 occasions and scored over 80 tries, including hat-tricks against Australia, France and New Zealand. He scored seven tries in a 1958 tour game against Western Australia in Perth playing at stand-off. What a player, what a man. Add that he played top class rugby league with seven rugby league Hall of Fame members, several Great Britain captains and many more greats; this gives some insight into Sully's quality.

He has been a resident in a care home for several years now and on my visits to him I have experienced warmth, humour, laughter, memories and great sadness. For the many fans who were lucky enough to have watched Mick and his team-mates in that good rugby league era he was a top man – Thanks for the Memories.

Sam Morton has had a lifetime's involvement with amateur rugby league, including playing and coaching at international level.

Maurice Bamford

While one could wax lyrical about the tries Sully scored, the defensive part of his game was special. His tackles were not all made on the touchline either, many were made in covering mode. One in particular is worth remembering. It was on a winter's afternoon at Headingley, in the first round of the Challenge Cup, Leeds versus Wigan, 1959, and a real tough cup tie it was. Leeds were in front by a three point try and the conversion, 5–0, when Derek Hallas, Leeds's speedy centre, was put clear from the half-way line in the centre of the field. It would be another try to Leeds and the goal kick would give Leeds the edge with a 10–0 lead, or so thought the Leeds faithful. Sully had other thoughts. Tearing across from the left wing, he gradually overhauled Hallas and with one final dive at the flying centre, brought him down heavily inches short of the line.

Wigan went on to win the game 12–5, but the tackle by Sully must have gone a long way to winning the game. Wigan went on to beat Hunslet, Halifax and then Leigh, in a hard-fought semi-final, 5–0 and went onto Wembley to beat Hull FC 30–13, in a one-sided final. But what if Sully had missed Hallas? Who knows?
(From *Play to Win – Rugby League Heroes* by Maurice Bamford)

Maurice Bamford played for Hull and Dewsbury before turning to coaching, where he coached Great Britain and various clubs, including Wigan and Leeds).

Aimee Sullivan

My granddad – where to begin? He is the greatest man the world has ever been blessed with. I have had the greatest and closest relationship with my grandparents, especially my granddad Mick Sullivan. I never really truly understood what influence he had on the rugby world, and how much of a legend he was, until I grew up. When I was young he was my big soft loving granddad who brought me breakfast in bed, let me play down in the cellar hammering nails into wood, playing dolls, and endless games of hide and seek.

Any chance I could get I would stay over at their house in school holidays, weekends, anytime. In one of the school holidays I was staying over, I didn't want him to go into the pub after he had got the shopping, so I decided to write a post-it note sticker and placed it on the back of his coat which he was totally unaware of. Unknown to him I had written "Don't serve me alcohol, I'm a naughty boy". He walked

142

through the whole of Dewsbury wearing it. With the amazing sense of humour he had, he found it hilarious. I found the post-it note sticker years later. He had kept it, I'm sure, to embarrass me when I was a lot older. That was the bond we had; no matter how cheeky I was he always laughed it off. When I used to hide the remote and leave him clues around the house leading to the television remote, he still found it hilarious. When we had to sort through his things before he went to his first care home he had kept all the stickers, all the notes, and letters I sent to him. I was forever writing letters to them, I think that has been the hardest part of his illness for me is not receiving any back. However, I'm extremely grateful and happy about the amazing memories I have from growing up, which make me smile and I'm so happy that I have had those special times with both of my grandparents, and have these small reminders about how much I loved them and I knew they loved me back.

I could write pages and pages about the things we used to get up too, as a pair we would drive my grandma insane sometimes 'you two are both as bad as each other' and then they would both laugh it off. Looking back now, I must have driven him crazy. We used to watch *Tarzan* movies or *Open all Hours* with a glass of milk and rich tea biscuits all the time over and over again. He was the most amazing granddad ever he would have them all ready and waiting for when I got there or have some more recorded on video for my next stay.

He has been a huge influence on my life, and made my childhood years filled with the happiest of memories of my granddad and grandma. I feel so lucky and privileged to have had him in my life and be so involved in everything I did. Even with his Alzheimer's he is still the gentle man which I grew up with, which just proves how amazing he is. Even with this awful illness there is still the true man he always has been. Recently at my uncle's wedding when his Alzheimer's has been at its worst, he was so polite and put his hand out to shake hands with everyone and smiled. It was such a proud moment to see him like this, but also the amount of people that wanted to come over and see him, to shake his hand and how happy they were to be able to speak to him.

I believe my own determination and aspiration to do anything in my life is down to him and my grandma Jean. I am so honoured to be his granddaughter and I hope to make him proud in everything I do.

The last word – Mike Stephenson

Every youngster has his hero, a person who you look up to and admire, the player you wanted to be when you passed the ball around the streets as a kid.

My hero was Mick Sullivan, a man who lived in the same town as me, Dewsbury, and despite not signing for his local team it didn't deter me from looking up to my idol as I followed his career at Huddersfield, Wigan and St Helens where he would eventually rise to stardom.

I even signed up as a young kid at the same junior club, Shaw Cross Boys Club where Mick honed his skills to near perfection and I considered it a treat to think I was changing into my boots in the same dressing rooms as the great winger had done many years before me.

By that time Mick had become a legend in our game both here and overseas, World Cup, Championship and Wembley winners medals and of course a British Lions tourist to Australia and New Zealand.

Not surprisingly with his talent enjoyed by many fans both here and down under it was impossible to think I was the only fan to class him has an hero for his character and playing ability had endeared him to many people.

I even signed professional forms to play at Dewsbury where Mick was by then the player-coach and became firm friends with a man who took time out to help and encourage a young kid like myself and many others who were trying to come to terms with a professional sport.

Again I felt honoured to be in the same dressing room as the great man himself a player who scored some sensational tries in his long career.

To try and emulate Mick Sullivan is I think an impossible task for he was fast, furious, tough and had a 'never say die' attitude that struck fear into any opponent he faced either as a winger, centre, stand-off and in his later years as a loose-forward.

Players always knew when Mick was around because his tough defence was second to none and even as a winger he could stun the opposition with ferocious tackling and yet he was a gentle guy off the field of play, his smile and his willingness to talk with young and old added to his legend tag, especially after he retired as a player.

Mick also played in Australia with a country side called Junee and I had the pleasure to visit this town many times where the legend of

Mick Sullivan still hangs on with pride and respect for his wonderful career in the Aussie 'Bush'.

Believe me, being a 'Pommie' down under leaves you no place to hide and many a player tried to get 'One over' the great Mick Sullivan of Great Britain fame, but they all came off second best.

I will never forget the time this gentleman gave to me over many years and the many happy hours we spent talking about the Greatest Game of All with the 'Legend' and I felt proud for him and his family as he finally was inducted into the Rugby League Hall of Fame.

Tina Turner perhaps summed it all up when she sang *Simply the Best*. I feel it was written with one Mick Sullivan in mind, for he is still just that ... 'The best'.

Mike Stephenson had a very successful rugby league career in Great Britain and Australia, including playing for Great Britain and winning the Championship with Dewsbury. He is now maybe better known as a co-commentator and pundit on Sky Sports.

Appendix: Statistics and records

Representative appearances

Great Britain – Tests

Sun 31 Oct 1954	Australia 13	Great Britain 28	Lyon	
Sun 7 Nov 1954	France 13	Great Britain 13	Toulouse	
Thu 11 Nov 1954	Great Britain 26	New Zealand 6	Bordeaux	
Sat 13 Nov 1954	France 12	Great Britain 16	Paris	
Sat 8 Oct 1955	Great Britain 25	New Zealand 6	Swinton	2 Tries
Sat 12 Nov 1955	Great Britain 27	New Zealand 12	Bradford	3 Tries
Sat 17 Dec 1955	Great Britain 13	New Zealand 28	Leeds	Try
Sat 17 Nov 1956	Great Britain 21	Australia 10	Wigan	Try
Sat 1 Dec 1956	Great Britain 9	Australia 22	Bradford	
Sat 15 Dec 1956	Great Britain 19	Australia 0	Swinton	Try
Sat 26 Jan 1957	Great Britain 45	France 12	Leeds	Try
Sun 3 Mar 1957	France 19	Great Britain 19	Toulouse	
Wed 10 Apr 1957	Great Britain 29	France 14	St Helens	2 Tries
Sat 15 Jun 1957	France 5	Great Britain 23	Sydney	2 Tries
Mon 17 Jun 1957	Australia 31	Great Britain 6	Sydney	
Tue 25 Jun 1957	Great Britain 21	New Zealand 29	Sydney	Try
Sun 3 Nov 1957	France 14	Great Britain 25	Toulouse	2 Tries
Sat 23 Nov 1957	Great Britain 44	France 15		Try
Sun 2 Mar 1958	France 9	Great Britain 23	Grenoble	Try
Sat 14 Jun 1958	Australia 25	Great Britain 8	Sydney	
Sat 5 Jul 1958	Australia 18	Great Britain 25	Brisbane	Try
Sat 19 Jul 1958	Australia 17	Great Britain 40	Sydney	3 Tries
Sat 26 Jul 1958	New Zealand 15	Great Britain 10	Auckland	Try
Sat 9 Aug 1958	New Zealand 15	Great Britain 32	Auckland	3 Tries
Sat 14 Mar 1959	Great Britain 50	France 15		
Sun 5 Apr 1959	France 24	Great Britain 15	Grenoble	
Sat 17 Oct 1959	Great Britain 14	Australia 22	Swinton	
Sat 21 Nov 1959	Great Britain 11	Australia 10	Leeds	
Sat 12 Dec 1959	Great Britain 18	Australia 12	Wigan	
Sun 6 Mar 1960	France 20	Great Britain 18	Toulouse	Try
Sat 26 Mar 1960	Great Britain 17	France 17		Try
Sat 24 Sep 1960	Great Britain 23	New Zealand 8	Bradford	
Sat 1 Oct 1960	Great Britain 33	France 7		
Sat 8 Oct 1960	Great Britain 10	Australia 3	Bradford	Try
Sun 11 Dec 1960	France 10	Great Britain 21	Bordeaux	Try
Sat 28 Jan 1961	Great Britain 27	France 8	St Helens	
Sat 21 Oct 1961	Great Britain 23	New Zealand 10	Bradford	2 Tries
Sat 4 Nov 1961	Great Britain 35	New Zealand 19	Swinton	2 Tries
Sat 17 Feb 1962	Great Britain 15	France 20	Wigan	Try
Sun 11 Mar 1962	France 23	Great Britain 13	Perpignan	Try
Sat 9 Jun 1962	Australia 12	Great Britain 31	Sydney	2 Tries
Sat 30 Jun 1962	Australia 10	Great Britain 17	Brisbane	
Sat 14 Jul 1962	Australia 18	Great Britain 17	Sydney	
Sat 28 Jul 1962	New Zealand 19	Great Britain 0	Auckland	
Sun 2 Dec 1962	France 17	Great Britain 12	Perpignan	
Sat 9 Nov 1963	Great Britain 12	Australia 50	Swinton	

Great Britain – Internationals

Sun 11 Dec 1955	France 17	Great Britain 5	Paris	Try
Wed 11 Apr 1956	Great Britain 18	France 10	Bradford	Try

England – Internationals
Mon 12 Sep 1955	England 16	Other Nationalities 33	Wigan	Try
Thu 10 May 1956	France 23	England 9	Lyon	Try
Sat 17 Nov 1962	England 18	France 6	Leeds	

NRL XIII – International
Sun 21 Oct 1956	France 17	NRL XIII 18	Marseilles	Try

Other representative matches
Wed 3 Oct 1956	Great Britain 26	Rest of League 23	Bradford	Try
Mon 12 Sep 1960	Great Britain 21	Rest of League 16	St Helens	
Mon 10 Oct 1960	Great Britain 33	Rest of World 27	Bradford	Try

English Services
Wed 13 Apr 1955	English Services 15	French Services 7	Leeds	
Sun 15 April 1956	French Services 18	English Services 10	Marseilles	

Yorkshire
Wed 21 Sep 1955	Yorkshire 17	New Zealand 33	Hull KR	2 Tries
Mon 26 Sep 1955	Lancashire 26	Yorkshire 10	Oldham	
Wed 19 Sep 1956	Cumberland 15	Yorkshire 14	Whitehaven	
Wed 11 Sep 1957	Yorkshire 27	Cumberland 18	Hull	Try
Mon 23 Sep 1957	Lancashire 11	Yorkshire 25	Widnes	2 Tries
Wed 24 Sep 1958	Yorkshire 35	Lancashire 19	Hull KR	2 Tries
Wed 29 Oct 1958	Lancashire 15	Yorkshire 16	Leigh	2 Tries
Wed 16 Sep 1959	Yorkshire 13	Cumberland 26	Hull	Try
Mon 28 Sep 1959	Yorkshire 47	Australia 15	York	Try
Wed 31 Aug 1960	Yorkshire 20	Lancashire 21	Wakefield	
Wed 14 Sep 1960	Cumberland 43	Yorkshire 19	Whitehaven	2 Tries
Wed 6 Sep 1961	Yorkshire 21	New Zealand 11	Hull KR	
Mon 11 Sep 1961	Yorkshire 8	Cumberland 23	Wakefield	
Mon 9 Oct 1961	Lancashire 14	Yorkshire 12	Leigh	

England amateur
Thu 7 Feb 1952	England 3	France 3	Broughton	

England Junior
Sun 27 Apr 1952	France 10	England 7	Avignon	
Sun 11 Apr 1954	France 2	England 13	Avignon	Try

Professional career summary
	Apps	Tries	Pts
Huddersfield	117	93	279
Wigan	125	84	252
St Helens	82	32	96
York	26	7	21
Dewsbury	40	2	6
Yorkshire	14	13	39
England	3	2	6
Great Britain	46	43	129
NRL	1	1	3
Great Britain tour matches	35	59	177
Totals	**489**	**336**	**1008**

Records from Sully's time with Junee are not available. The above does not include club friendly matches or testimonial games.

Tour matches

1957 (World Cup in bold)

Sun 9 Jun	W. Australia 5	Great Britain 66	Perth	7 Tries
Sat 15 Jun	**France 5**	**Great Britain 23**	**Sydney**	2 Tries
Mon 17 Jun	**Australia 31**	**Great Britain 6**	**Sydney**	
Tue 25 Jun	**Great Britain 21**	**New Zealand 29**	**Sydney**	Try
Mon 1 Jul	Queensland 5	Great Britain 44	Brisbane	3 Tries
Sat 6 Jul	French XIII 12	Great Britain 26	Auckland	
Mon 8 Jul	New Zealand 31	N. Hemisphere 34	Auckland	Try
Sat 20 Jul	French XIII 41	Great Britain 61	Benoni	3 Tries
Wed 24 Jul	French XIII 11	Great Britain 32	Durban	2 Tries
Sat 27 Jul	French XIII 11	Great Britain 69	East London	Try

Played 10 matches, scoring 20 tries

1958 (Test matches in bold)

Sun 18 May	S. Districts 18	Great Britain 36	Wollongong	2 Tries
Wed 21 May	W. Districts 24	Great Britain 24	Orange	Try
Sat 24 May	Newcastle 16	Great Britain 35	Newcastle	Try
Wed 28 May	Northern NSW 17	Great Britain 27	Tamworth	2 Tries
Sat 31 May	Sydney 15	Great Britain 20	Sydney	
Sat 7 Jun	NSW 10	Great Britain 19	Sydney	2 Tries
Sat 14 Jun	**Australia 25**	**Great Britain 8**	**Sydney**	
Sat 21 Jun	Queensland 19	Great Britain 36	Brisbane	2 Tries
Sat 5 Jul	**Australia 18**	**Great Britain 25**	**Brisbane**	**Try**
Sat 19 Jul	**Australia 17**	**Great Britain 40**	**Sydney**	**3 Tries**
Sat 26 Jul	**New Zealand 15**	**Great Britain 10**	**Auckland**	**Try**
Mon 28 Jul	Taranaki 8	Great Britain 67	New Plymouth	6 Tries
Wed 30 Jul	Wellington 20	Great Britain 62	Wellington	3 Tries
Sat 2 Aug	Canterbury 21	Great Britain 41	Christchurch	3 Tries
Sun 3 Aug	West Coast 2	Great Britain 19	Greymouth	
Wed 6 Aug	Comb Provinces 3	Great Britain 72	Palmerston N	Try
Sat 9 Aug	**New Zealand 15**	**Great Britain 32**	**Auckland**	**3 Tries**
Thu 14 Aug	Sydney Colts 11	Great Britain 19	Sydney	
Sun 24 Aug	W. Australia 23	Great Britain 69	Perth	7 Tries

Played 19 matches, scoring 38 tries

1962 (Test matches in bold)

Sun 20 May	W. Australia 12	Great Britain 39	Perth	3 Tries
Wed 23 May	Riverina 7	Great Britain 34	Wagga Wagga	Try
Sat 2 Jun	NSW 28	Great Britain 33	Sydney	Try
Sat 9 Jun	**Australia 12**	**Great Britain 31**	**Sydney**	**2 Tries**
Sun 10 Jun	N. Coast NSW 13	Great Britain 33	Lismore	
Wed 13 Jun	Brisbane 14	Great Britain 16	Brisbane	2 Tries
Sat 16 Jun	Queensland 17	Great Britain 22	Brisbane	
Wed 20 Jun	Ctrl Queensland 8	Great Britain 55	Rockhampton	
Sat 23 Jun	Far N. Qld 31	Great Britain 33	Cairns (sub)	
Sun 24 Jun	N. Queensland 14	Great Britain 47	Townsville	
Sat 30 Jun	**Australia 10**	**Great Britain 17**	**Brisbane**	
Sat 7 Jul	NSW 5	Great Britain 20	Sydney	Try
Sun 8 Jul	S. NSW 18	Great Britain 10	Wollongong	
Sat 14 Jul	**Australia 18**	**Great Britain 17**	**Sydney**	
Wed 25 Jul	Waikato 20	Great Britain 59	Huntly	Try
Sat 28 Jul	**New Zealand 19**	**Great Britain 0**	**Auckland**	
Sat 4 Aug	New Zealand XIII 17	Great Britain 31	Christchurch	2 Tries

| Sun 5 Aug | West Coast 8 | Great Britain 66 | Greymouth | Try |
| Tue 7 Aug | Bay of Plenty 14 | Great Britain 81 | Rotorua | |

Played 19 matches (one as substitute), scoring 14 tries

South Africa

Thu 23 Aug	RLSA 30	Great Britain 49	Pretoria	
Sat 25 Aug	RLSA 33	Great Britain 39	Durban	2 tries
Fri 31 Aug	RLSA 23	Great Britain 45	Johannesburg	3 tries

Played 3 matches, scoring 5 tries

Club appearances

Unless stated all matches are part of the Northern Rugby League competition.
Scores are listed with Sullivan's club's first.

Legend

CH: Championship	TM: Tour match
CC: Challenge Cup	WD: Western Division
ED: Eastern Division	YC: Yorkshire Cup
LC: Lancashire Cup	

1952–53 Huddersfield

Sat 4 Oct 52	Dewsbury (a)	21–6	2 Tries	
Thu 16 Oct 52	Halifax (a)	15–5	2 Tries	YCSFR
Sat 18 Oct 52	Doncaster (a)	9–25		
Sat 22 Nov 52	York (a)	20–7		
Sat 24 Jan 53	Hull (a)	11–27	Try	
Sat 21 Mar 53	Wakefield T (a)	19–7		
Sat 11 Apr 53	Leeds (a)	5–12		
Tue 28 Apr 53	Castleford	38–5	2 Tries	
Wed 17 Jun 53	Keighley (Blackpool)	39–10	Try	F
Fri 19 Jun 53	Barrow (Blackpool)	7–53	Try	F

1953–54 Huddersfield

Sat 10 Oct 53	Leigh (h)	25–19	Try	
Sat 17 Oct 53	Dewsbury (a)	25–13		
Sat 28 Nov 53	Wakefield T (a)	18–26		
Sat 23 Jan 54	Hunslet (h)	28–2		
Mon 15 Feb 54	Belle Vue R (a)	20–15		CCR1 Leg 1
Fri 30 Apr 54	Hull (a)	18–4		F

1954–55 Huddersfield

Sat 7 Aug 54	Halifax (a)	3–10		F
Sat 14 Aug 54	Castleford (a)	43–17	Try	
Sat 21 Aug 54	Doncaster (a)	26–12		
Wed 25 Aug 54	Dewsbury (h)	39–8		
Sat 28 Aug 54	Hull KR (h)	39–7		
Tue 31 Aug 54	Keighley (a)	36–26	2 Tries	
Sat 4 Sep 54	Bramley (a)	9–14		
Sat 11 Sep 54	Keighley (h)	40–17		YCR1
Sat 18 Sep 54	Featherstone R (h)	23–14	Try	
Tue 21 Sep 54	Hull (h)	7–7	Try	YCR2
Thu 23 Sep 54	Hull (a)	13–22	Try	YCR2R
Sat 25 Sep 54	St Helens (a)	7–20		
Sat 2 Oct 54	Hunslet (h)	30–16	Try	
Sat 9 Oct 54	Hull (a)	17–23		

Date	Opponent	Score	Tries	Note
Sat 16 Oct 54	York (h)	25–22	Try	
Sat 23 Oct 54	Hull KR (a)	31–12		
Sat 20 Nov 54	Leigh (a)	16–21		
Sat 27 Nov 54	Wakefield T (h)	25–8	Try	
Sat 4 Dec 54	Wakefield T (a)	25–6		
Sat 11 Dec 54	Bradford N (h)	22–10		
Sat 25 Dec 54	Halifax (h)	0–15		
Mon 27 Dec 54	Halifax (a)	3–7		
Tue 28 Dec 54	Bramley (h)	22–18		
Sat 1 Jan 55	Hunslet (a)	10–20		
Sat 29 Jan 55	Hull (h)	32–15	2 Tries	
Sat 9 Apr 55	Workington T (h)	44–13	Try	
Mon 11 Apr 55	St Helens (h)	35–11	Try	
Tue 12 Apr 55	Featherstone R (a)	19–20		
Sat 23 Apr 55	Doncaster (h)	42–14	Try	
Sat 7 May 55	Workington T (a)	8–33		

1955–56 Huddersfield

Date	Opponent	Score	Tries	Note
Sat 13 Aug 55	Halifax (h)	29–6	3 Tries	F
Sat 20 Aug 55	Rochdale H (a)	14–24	Try	
Mon 22 Aug 55	Castleford (h)	30–6		
Sat 27 Aug 55	Featherstone R (a)	9–26		YCR1
Wed 31 Aug 55	Keighley (h)	48–14	3 Tries	
Sat 3 Sep 55	Batley (a)	36–9		
Sat 10 Sep 55	Bramley (h)	46–7	Try	
Sat 17 Sep 55	Leigh (a)	11–38		
Sat 24 Sep 55	Featherstone R (h)	18–25		
Wed 28 Sep 55	Wigan (London)	33–11	Try	ITV RLC
Sat 1 Oct 55	York (a)	12–21		
Sat 15 Oct 55	Warrington (a)	11–27		
Sat 22 Oct 55	New Zealand (h)	25–16	2 Tries	
Sat 29 Oct 55	Bradford N (a)	2–14		
Sat 5 Nov 55	York (h)	10–0	Try	
Sat 19 Nov 55	Warrington (h)	16–20	2 Tries	
Sat 26 Nov 55	Leeds (a)	18–14	Try	
Sat 3 Dec 55	Dewsbury (h)	16–9	Try	
Sat 24 Dec 55	Bramley (a)	10–19		
Mon 26 Dec 55	Halifax (h)	3–22		
Tue 27 Dec 55	Halifax (a)	0–34		
Sat 31 Dec 55	Hull KR (h)	34–8	3 Tries	
Sat 21 Jan 56	Doncaster (h)	24–5		
Sat 11 Feb 56	Whitehaven (h)	8–4	2 Tries	CCR1
Sat 3 Mar 56	Swinton (a)	8–6	Try	CCR2
Sat 17 Mar 56	Castleford (a)	41–5	2 Tries	
Tue 3 Apr 56	Featherstone R (a)	7–7	Try	
Sat 7 Apr 56	Bradford N (h)	7–11	Try	
Tue 10 Apr 56	Doncaster (a)	21–5	2 Tries	
Wed 18 Apr 56	Wakefield T (h)	2–26	Try	

1956–57 Huddersfield

Date	Opponent	Score	Tries	Note
Mon 13 Aug 56	Halifax (a)	13–23		F
Sat 18 Aug 56	Castleford (h)	24–6	2 Tries	
Wed 29 Aug 56	Bradford N (h)	45–10	3 Tries	
Sat 1 Sep 56	Batley (h)	41–2	3 Tries	YCR1
Sat 8 Sep 56	Hull (h)	26–5	Try	
Mon 10 Sep 56	Wakefield T (a)	11–13		YCR2

150

Sat 15 Sep 56	Barrow (a)	15–24	Try	
Sat 22 Sep 56	Leeds (h)	26–12	Try	
Sat 29 Sep 56	Castleford (a)	32–17	Try	
Sat 6 Oct 56	Warrington (a)	7–20		
Sat 13 Oct 56	Bramley (h)	24–13	Try	
Sat 27 Oct 56	Featherstone R (h)	10–6	Try	
Sat 3 Nov 56	Bramley (a)	24–10	Try	
Sat 10 Nov 56	Australia (h)	10–20	Try	TM
Sat 24 Nov 56	Batley (h)	9–13		
Sat 8 Dec 56	Wakefield T (h)	22–6	Try	
Sat 22 Dec 56	Keighley (h)	7–10		
Tue 25 Dec 56	Halifax (h)	13–17		
Sat 19 Jan 57	Hull KR (h)	10–13		
Sat 2 Feb 57	Leeds (a)	20–24		
Wed 13 Feb 57	Swinton (h)	5–0	Try	CCR1R
Sat 16 Feb 57	Dewsbury (h)	27–10	2 Tries	
Sat 23 Feb 57	Salford (a)	6–2		CCR2
Sat 9 Mar 57	Barrow (a)	0–10		CCR3
Sat 16 Mar 57	Wigan (h)	10–20		
Sat 23 Mar 57	St Helens (h)	9–10	Try	
Sat 30 Mar 57	Hunslet (h)	8–20	Try	
Wed 3 Apr 57	Halifax (a)	10–5		
Sat 6 Apr 57	Wigan (a)	13–8		
Sat 20 Apr 57	Hull KR (a)	14–16	Try	
Tue 23 Apr 57	Featherstone R (a)	26–18	Try	
Sat 27 Apr 57	Wakefield T (a)	14–20	2 Tries	

1957–58 Huddersfield

Sat 10 Aug 57	Halifax (h)	56–19	3 Tries	F
Sat 17 Aug 57	Bradford N (h)	33–15	Try	
Wed 21 Aug 57	St Helens (a)	8–28		
Sat 24 Aug 57	Wigan (a)	7–25		
Wed 28 Aug 57	Leeds (h)	16–11		
Sat 31 Aug 57	Batley (h)	68–19	6 Tries	YCR1
Mon 2 Sep 57	Oldham (h)	12–38		
Sat 7 Sep 57	Barrow (a)	10–13	Try	
Sat 14 Sep 57	York (h)	17–11	Try	
Mon 16 Sep 57	Wakefield T (a)	13–10	Try	YCR2
Sat 21 Sep 57	Castleford (h)	23–7	4 Tries	
Sat 28 Sep 57	Wakefield T (a)	9–23	2 Tries	
Wed 2 Oct 57	Leeds (h)	14–2	Try	YCSF
Sat 5 Oct 57	St Helens (h)	13–35	Try	
Sat 12 Oct 57	Hull KR (a)	20–20	Try	
Sat 19 Oct 57	York (n)	15–8		YCF

1957–58 Wigan

Sat 26 Oct 57	Leigh (h)	7–9		
Sat 16 Nov 57	Leeds (a)	5–17		
Sat 30 Nov 57	Wakefield T (h)	23–10	Try	
Sat 7 Dec 57	Workington T (a)	3–8		
Sat 14 Dec 57	Widnes (h)	18–5	Try	
Sat 21 Dec 57	Hull (a)	5–37		
Wed 25 Dec 57	Salford (a)	14–7		
Thu 26 Dec 57	St Helens (h)	9–12		
Sat 28 Dec 57	Blackpool B (h)	30–13		
Wed 1 Jan 58	Warrington (h)	22–13		

Sat 4 Jan 58	Halifax (a)	16–8	Try	
Sat 11 Jan 58	Rochdale H (h)	22–10		
Sat 1 Feb 58	Oldham (h)	6–9		
Sat 8 Feb 58	Whitehaven (h)	39–10	3 Tries	CCR1
Sat 15 Feb 58	Hunslet (h)	24–0	Try	
Sat 22 Feb 58	Wakefield T (a)	11–5		CCR2
Sat 8 Mar 58	Oldham (a)	8–0		CCR3
Sat 15 Mar 58	Blackpool B (a)	13–2		
Wed 19 Mar 58	Whitehaven (h)	28–6	3 Tries	
Sat 22 Mar 58	Halifax (h)	20–8	Try	
Sat 29 Mar 58	Rochdale H (n)	5–3	Try	CCSF
Fri 4 Apr 58	St Helens (a)	7–32		
Sat 5 Apr 58	Oldham (a)	7–19	Try	
Mon 7 Apr 58	Swinton (h)	26–7	Try	
Sat 12 Apr 58	Salford (h)	42–2	4 Tries	
Wed 16 Apr 58	Huddersfield (a)	31–11	2 Tries	
Wed 19 Apr 58	Barrow (a)	25–12	Try	
Sat 23 Apr 58	Leigh (a)	23–14		
Sat 10 May 58	Workington T (n)	13–9	Try	CCF

1958–59 Wigan

Sat 30 Aug 58	Swinton (a)	31–12		LCR1
Sat 6 Sep 58	Barrow (h)	49–16		
Sat 13 Sep 58	Hull (a)	15–34	2 Tries	
Tue 16 Sep 58	Oldham (a)	7–19		LCR2
Sat 20 Sep 58	Featherstone R (h)	46–5	2 Tries	
Sat 27 Sep 58	Swinton (h)	24–8		
Sat 4 Oct 58	Rochdale H (a)	23–16		
Sat 11 Oct 58	Featherstone R (a)	6–13		
Sat 18 Oct 58	Whitehaven (h)	39–16		
Sat 25 Oct 58	Leeds (a)	8–17	Try	
Sat 1 Nov 58	Leigh (h)	26–12	Try	
Sat 8 Nov 58	Hunslet (a)	21–29		
Sat 15 Nov 58	Hull (h)	31–7		
Sat 22 Nov 58	Barrow (a)	23–17	Try	
Sat 29 Nov 58	Oldham (h)	19–7		
Sat 6 Dec 58	Swinton (a)	22–7	2 Tries	
Sat 13 Dec 58	Halifax (h)	27–7		
Sat 20 Dec 58	Oldham (a)	18–21	2 Tries	
Thu 25 Dec 58	Salford (h)	31–14	2 Tries	
Fri 26 Dec 58	St Helens (a)	9–13		
Sat 27 Dec 58	Leigh (a)	25–15		
Thu 1 Jan 59	Warrington (h)	24–16	Try	
Sat 3 Jan 59	Wakefield T (h)	22–5		
Sat 24 Jan 59	Liverpool C (a)	36–18	Try	
Sat 31 Jan 59	Liverpool C (h)	45–7	Try	
Sat 7 Feb 59	Widnes (h)	7–11		
Sat 14 Feb 59	Warrington (a)	18–5		
Sat 21 Feb 59	Leeds (h)	12–5		CCR1
Sat 28 Feb 59	Blackpool B (h)	29–11	Try	

152

Sat 7 Mar 59	Hunslet (h)	22–4		CCR2
Sat 21 Mar 59	Halifax (a)	26–0	2 Tries	CCR3
Fri 27 Mar 59	St Helens (h)	19–14		
Sat 28 Mar 59	Workington T (a)	13–5	Try	
Mon 30 Mar 59	Salford (a)	38–15	2 Tries	
Sat 11 Apr 59	Leigh (n)	5–0	Try	CCSF
Wed 15 Apr 59	Blackpool B (a)	15–12		
Sat 22 Apr 59	Wakefield T (a)	13–12	Try	
Tue 25 Apr 59	Workington T (h)	31–16	Try	
Thu 27 Apr 59	Widnes (a)	10–5	Try	
Sat 2 May 59	Hunslet (a)	11–22		CHSF
Sat 9 May 59	Hull (n)	30–13	Try	CCF

1959–60 Wigan

Sat 8 Aug 59	Warrington (h)	31–22		F
Sat 15 Aug 59	Wakefield T (a)	14–21	Try	
Wed 19 Aug 59	Widnes (h)	16–12		
Sat 22 Aug 59	Swinton (h)	37–6		
Wed 26 Aug 59	Leigh (a)	22–22	2 Tries	
Sat 29 Aug 59	Rochdale H (h)	39–20	2 Tries	LCR1
Sat 5 Sep 59	Wakefield T (h)	19–27	Try	
Mon 7 Sep 59	Salford (h)	39–15		LCR2
Tue 15 Sep	Warrington (h)	13–15		LCSF
Sat 19 Sep 59	Leeds (a)	29–13	Try	
Sat 26 Sep 59	Rochdale H (h)	8–18		
Sat 3 Oct 59	Warrington (a)	6–16		
Sat 10 Oct 59	Whitehaven (h)	31–12	Try	
Sat 24 Oct 59	Liverpool C (h)	17–6	Try	
Sat 31 Oct 59	Dewsbury (a)	35–7		
Sat 14 Nov 59	Australia (h)	16–9		TM
Sat 28 Nov 59	Halifax (a)	20–21		
Sat 5 Dec 59	Oldham (h)	27–7		
Sat 26 Dec 59	St Helens (h)	7–19		
Mon 28 Dec 59	Salford (a)	20–13		
Fri 1 Jan 60	Warrington (h)	34–5		
Sat 2 Jan 60	Hunslet (a)	10–15		
Sat 9 Jan 60	Workington T (h)	7–11		
Sat 16 Jan 60	Whitehaven (a)	7–7	Try	
Sat 23 Jan 60	Leigh (h)	12–10	2 Tries	
Sat 6 Feb 60	Barrow (h)	43–3	4 Tries	
Sat 13 Feb 60	Hunslet (a)	9–5		CCR1
Sat 20 Feb 60	Leeds (h)	9–0		
Sat 27 Feb 60	Leeds (h)	14–11	Try	CCR2
Sat 12 Mar 60	Oldham (a)	11–10	Try	
Sat 19 Mar 60	Hull (a)	8–12		CCR3
Sat 2 Apr 60	Widnes (a)	42–9	2 Tries	
Sat 9 Apr 60	Dewsbury (h)	58–6	3 Tries	
Mon 11 Apr 60	Barrow (a)	11–0		

153

Fri 15 Apr 60	St Helens (a)	4–12		
Sat 16 Apr 60	Liverpool C (a)	39–20	Try	
Mon 18 Apr 60	Salford (h)	38–13	Try	
Sat 23 Apr 60	Swinton (a)	16–14		
Sat 30 Apr 60	Blackpool B (a)	30–7	Try	
Sat 7 May 60	St Helens (a)	19–9		CHSF

1960–61 Wigan

Wed 17 Aug 60	Leigh (a)	25–9		
Sat 20 Aug 60	Hull (a)	30–9		
Mon 22 Aug 60	Whitehaven (h)	25–11	Try	
Sat 27 Aug 60	Oldham (h)	19–5	Try	LCR1
Thu 1 Sep 60	Barrow (a)	24–12		
Sat 3 Sep 60	Blackpool B (a)	24–12		
Sat 17 Sep 60	Whitehaven (a)	2–14		
Sat 15 Oct 60	Leigh (h)	15–17	2 Tries	
Sat 22 Oct 60	St Helens (a)	6–11		
Sat 5 Nov 60	Hunslet (a)	10–3	Try	
Sat 12 Nov 60	Wakefield T (a)	7–12	Try	
Sat 19 Nov 60	Blackpool B (h)	16–11	Try	
Sat 26 Nov 60	Widnes (a)	3–5		
Sat 3 Dec 60	Hull (h)	22–15		
Sat 17 Dec 60	Swinton (h)	4–16		
Sat 7 Jan 61	Swinton (a)	12–10		

1960–61 St Helens

Mon 16 Jan 61	Hull (h)	22–15	Try	
Sat 21 Jan 61	Whitehaven (a)	15–11		
Sat 4 Feb 61	Warrington (h)	7–8		
Sat 11 Feb 61	Widnes (h)	5–5		CCR1
Thu 16 Feb 61	Widnes (a)	29–10	Try	CCR1R
Sat 18 Feb 61	Widnes (h)	44–7	Try	
Sat 25 Feb 61	Castleford (a)	18–10	Try	CCR2
Tue 20 Mar 61	Barrow (h)	31–2		
Sat 25 Mar 61	Salford (h)	45–2		
Mon 27 Mar 61	Wakefield T (a)	2–4		
Fri 31 Mar 61	Wigan (a)	2–12		
Sat 1 Apr 61	Workington T (a)	11–12		
Mon 3 Apr 61	Swinton (h)	3–10		
Sat 8 Apr 61	Hull (a)	9–4		
Sat 15 Apr 61	Hull (n)	26–9		CCSF
Sat 22 Apr 61	Featherstone R (a)	11–28		
Tue 25 Apr 61	Blackpool B (h)	28–4		
Sat 29 Apr 61	Featherstone R (h)	38–0	Try	
Sat 6 May 61	Leeds (a)	4–11		CHSF
Sat 13 May 61	Wigan (n)	12–6		CCF

154

1961–62 St Helens

Date	Opponent	Score	Tries	Notes
Sat 12 Aug 61	Liverpool C (h)	29–14		F
Sat 19 Aug 61	Leeds (h)	20–5	Try	
Sat 26 Aug 61	Swinton (a)	6–15		
Sat 2 Sep 61	Leigh (h)	43–8	Try	LCR1
Sat 9 Sep 61	Salford (a)	24–7		
Sat 16 Sep 61	Whitehaven (h)	44–0		
Sat 23 Sep 61	Barrow (a)	34–2		
Sat 30 Sep 61	Hull (h)	22–25		
Mon 2 Oct 61	Oldham (a)	30–7	2 Tries	LCR2
Sat 7 Oct 61	Whitehaven (a)	10–3		
Tue 10 Oct 61	Salford (h)	21–2		LCR3
Sat 14 Oct 61	New Zealand (h)	25–10		TM
Sat 28 Oct 61	Warrington (a)	7–11		
Sat 11 Nov 61	Swinton (n)	25–9	Try	LCF
Sat 18 Nov 61	Widnes (a)	12–13		
Sat 25 Nov 61	Workington T (h)	16–7	Try	
Sat 2 Dec 61	Hull KR (a)	5–12		
Sat 9 Dec 61	Wakefield T (a)	10–12		
Sat 16 Dec 61	Oldham (h)	8–9		
Sat 6 Jan 62	Barrow (h)	30–6		
Sat 13 Jan 62	Leeds (a)	3–20		
Sat 3 Feb 62	Huddersfield (h)	36–5	5 Tries	
Sat 10 Feb 62	Salford (a)	15–2		CCR1
Sat 24 Feb 62	Leigh (a)	6–7		
Sat 3 Mar 62	Huddersfield (h)	2–13		CCR2
Sat 24 Mar 62	Widnes (h)	13–8		
Sat 31 Mar 62	Swinton (h)	5–2		
Tue 3 Apr 62	Hull KR (h)	27–2		
Sat 7 Apr 62	Hull (a)	12–8		
Mon 9 Apr 62	Leigh (h)	42–4	Try	
Sat 14 Apr 62	Blackpool B (a)	15–2	2 Tries	
Fri 20 Apr 62	Wigan (h)	16–18	Try	

1962–63 St Helens

Date	Opponent	Score	Tries	Notes
Sat 22 Sep 62	Liverpool C (h)	32–3	Try	WD
Sat 29 Sep 62	Blackpool B (a)	12–12		WD
Wed 2 Oct 62	Oldham (a)	10–8		LCSF
Wed 9 Oct 62	Widnes (h)	9–10		WDSF
Sat 13 Oct 62	Castleford (h)	10–10		
Sat 20 Oct 62	Huddersfield (a)	22–9		
Sat 27 Oct 62	Swinton (n)	7–4		LCF
Sat 10 Nov 62	Warrington (h)	2–4		
Sat 24 Nov 62	Huddersfield (h)	36–3		
Sat 8 Dec 62	Leeds (h)	13–6		
Sat 15 Dec 62	Wakefield T (a)	7–10		
Sat 22 Dec 62	Hull (h)	27–14		
Sat 9 Mar 63	Hull KR (a)	2–3		
Mon 11 Mar 63	Halifax (a)	2–9		CCR1
Sat 23 Mar 63	Bramley (h)	38–0	3 Tries	
Tue 26 Mar 63	Wigan (h)	20–11		
Sat 30 Mar 63	Featherstone R (a)	17–10	Try	
Mon 1 Apr 63	Workington T (h)	29–0	2 Tries	
Sat 6 Apr 63	Halifax (h)	33–3	Try	
Fri 12 Apr 63	Wigan (a)	24–4	Try	
Sat 13 Apr 63	Swinton (a)	8–9		

Mon 15 Apr 63	Swinton (h)	9–24		
Sat 20 Apr 63	Featherstone R (h)	18–5		
Mon 29 Apr 63	Wakefield T (h)	15–16		
Wed 4 May 63	Widnes (a)	25–2		
Mon 6 May 63	Oldham (h)	22–8	Try	
Mon 13 May 63	Widnes (h)	14–6		
Sat 18 May 63	Bramley (a)	21–9		
Thu 23 May 63	Halifax (a)	33–5	Try	
Mon 27 May 63	Hull KR (h)	16–15		
Thu 30 May 63	Oldham (a)	24–9	Try	

1963–64 York

Sat 24 Aug 63	Salford (a)	21–23	2 Tries	
Wed 28 Aug 63	Liverpool C (h)	10–11		
Sat 31 Aug 63	Leigh (h)	7–25		
Wed 4 Sep 63	Bramley (a)	5–20		
Sat 7 Sep 63	Doncaster (a)	2–3		YCR1
Wed 11 Sep 63	Hull (h)	17–7		ED
Sat 5 Oct 63	Halifax (a)	9–23	Try	ED
Sat 12 Oct 63	Blackpool B (a)	10–17		
Sat 19 Oct 63	Whitehaven (h)	36–5		
Sat 2 Nov 63	Blackpool B (h)	7–5		
Sat 16 Nov 63	Barrow (a)	0–8		
23 Nov 63	Dewsbury (a)	9–12		
Sat 7 Dec 63	Liverpool C (a)	9–5	2 Tries	
Sat 14 Dec 63	Rochdale H (h)	34–5		
Sat 4 Jan 64	Hull KR (h)	11–13		ED
Sat 11 Jan 64	Salford (h)	14–8		
Sat 25 Jan 64	Leigh (a)	7–12	Try	
Sat 8 Feb 64	Bramley (h)	5–2		CCR1
Sat 29 Feb 64	Hull KR (h)	7–23	Try	CCR2
Mon 20 Apr 64	Featherstone R (h)	13–13		ED
Thu 23 Apr 64	Doncaster (a)	3–10		
Sat 25 Apr 64	Barrow (h)	35–17		

1964–65 York

Sat 22 Aug 64	Barrow (a)	7–24	
Wed 26 Aug 64	Hull (h)	4–8	
Sat 29 Aug 64	Dewsbury (h)	23–15	
Tue 1 Sep 64	Rochdale H (a)	12–23	

1964–65 Dewsbury

Sat 27 Mar 65	Bramley (a)	2–2	
Tue 30 Mar 65	Halifax (a)	5–27	
Sat 3 Apr 65	Leeds (h)	9–3	
Tue 6 Apr 65	Halifax (h)	13–7	Try
Tue 13 Apr 65	Batley (h)	12–9	
Fri 16 Apr 65	Batley (a)	9–7	
Sat 17 Apr 65	Hunslet (h)	5–10	
Mon 19 Apr 65	Oldham (a)	6–3	
Thu 21 Apr 65	Keighley (a)	16–7	

1965–66 Dewsbury

Sat 21 Aug 65	Salford (a)	11–21	
Sat 4 Sep 65	Huddersfield (h)	4–27	YCR1
Sat 11 Sep 65	Bradford N (a)	2–11	

Sat 18 Sep 65	Salford (h)	16–15	Try
Fri 24 Sep 65	Hull KR (a)	12–27	
Sat 2 Oct 65	Hull KR (h)	19–8	
Fri 22 Oct 65	Castleford (a)	0–15	
Sat 30 Oct 65	Hull (h)	9–5	
Sat 6 Nov 65	Halifax (a)	9–15	
Sat 13 Nov 65	Bradford N (h)	14–3	
Sat 20 Nov 65	Bramley (a)	3–8	
Sat 4 Dec 65	Featherstone R (a)	2–4	
Sat 18 Dec 65	Doncaster (h)	8–2	
Sat 25 Dec 65	Batley (h)	8–2	
Sat 1 Jan 66	Barrow (h)	2–11	
Sat 8 Jan 66	Keighley (a)	12–24	
Sat 29 Jan 66	Castleford (h)	2–9	
Sat 5 Feb 66	Leeds (a)	2–18	
Sat 12 Feb 66	Wakefield T (a)	5–13	
Sat 26 Feb 66	Keighley (a)	5–4	CCR1
Sat 5 Mar 66	Batley (a)	9–9	
Sat 12 Mar 66	Featherstone R (h)	9–15	
Sat 19 Mar 66	Barrow (h)	23–15	CCR2
Sat 26 Mar 66	Keighley (h)	11–5	
Tue 5 Apr 66	Huddersfield (h)	8–2	CCR3
Sat 9 Apr 66	York (h)	3–9	
Sat 16 Apr 66	St Helens (n)	5–12	CCSF

1966–67 Dewsbury

Sat 27 Aug 66	Bradford N (h)	2–12	
Mon 29 Aug 66	Hunslet (a)	0–15	
Sat 3 Sep 66	Wakefield T (h)	13–13	YCR1
Mon 5 Sep 66	Wakefield T (a)	11–18	YCR1R

Other books from London League Publications Ltd:

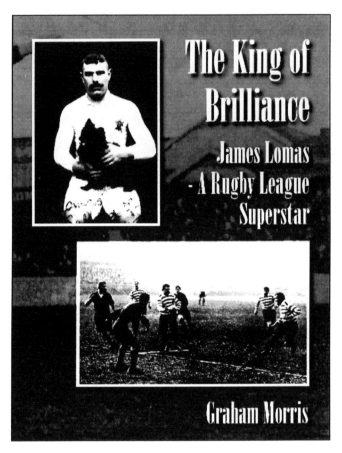

The King of Brilliance: Great book about one of the sport's genuine legends. James Lomas played for Bramley, Salford, Oldham and York, and won representative honours for Lancashire, Cumberland, England and Great Britain. He captained the first Lions team to tour Australia and New Zealand in 1910. This is the first biography of him.
Published in October 2011 at £16.95 (hardback). Special offer: £9.95 post free in the UK available direct from London League Publications Ltd.
All our books can be ordered from any bookshop @ full price. To order direct from London League Publications Ltd visit our website: www.llpshop.co.uk or write to LLP, PO Box 65784, London NW2 9NS (cheques payable to London League Publications Ltd).
Most of our books are available as E-Books for Kindle from Amazon.

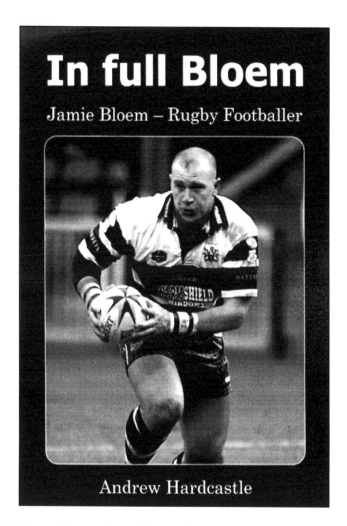

In full Bloem

Jamie Bloem – Rugby Footballer

Andrew Hardcastle

In full Bloem: The explosive biography of South African rugby league star Jamie Bloem, current referee and former Castleford, Oldham, Halifax, Widnes, Doncaster and Huddersfield player. He also played regularly for South Africa, and was capped by Scotland.
Published in February 2013 @ £14.95 (hardback), just £8.95 post free in the UK direct from London League Publications Ltd.

All our books can be ordered from any bookshop @ full price. To order direct from London League Publications Ltd visit our website: www.llpshop.co.uk or write to LLP, PO Box 65784, London NW2 9NS (cheques payable to London League Publications Ltd). Most of our books are available as E-Books for Kindle from Amazon.

The collapse of Bradford Northern RLFC in December 1963 sent shock waves throughout rugby league in Great Britain. Northern were the first team to appear in three successive Wembley Cup finals, from 1947 to 1949, and were top of the league at the start of the 1954–55 season.

However, by December 1963, this once proud club had sunk to the bottom of the league table and withdrew from the competition in mid-season. It was the first time since the 1920s that a team had pulled out of the league without completing their fixtures. Their membership of the RFL was terminated and that season's record was expunged.

"Come on Northern"

The fall and rise of Bradford Northern RLFC 1954 to 1965

Trevor Delaney

No club in the game's history had fallen from the heights quite like the old Northern. Their subsequent re-entry to the league was a great achievement for two men of vision – former Odsal greats, Trevor Foster and Joe Phillips.

Trevor Delaney, recalls this period in the club's turbulent history. "Come on Northern" is an essential read for everyone interested in rugby league.

Available for just £13.00 post free in the UK direct from London League Publications Ltd. Credit card orders via www.llpshop.co.uk; payment by cheque to PO Box 65784, London NW2 9NS. Available in bookshops at £13.95.

Also available as an E-Book for Kindle from Amazon.

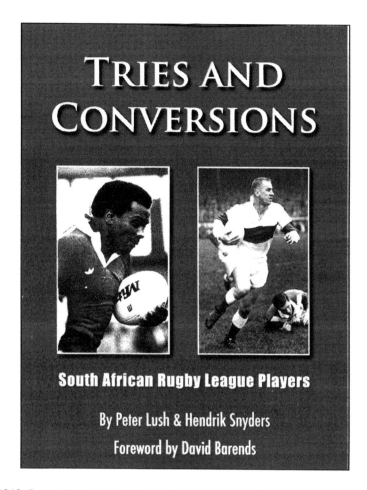

TRIES AND CONVERSIONS

South African Rugby League Players

By Peter Lush & Hendrik Snyders

Foreword by David Barends

In 1910, James Megson and William Mart became the first native-born South Africans to sign for British rugby league clubs. Since then, South African players have made a significant contribution to rugby league. This book is the first comprehensive study of their contribution to rugby league. It covers players who played in Great Britain and Australia. Some were very successful, such as Attie van Heerden and George van Rooyen in the 1920s, Tom van Vollenhoven, Alan Skene, Jan Prinsloo and Len Killeen in the 1950s and 1960s, and Mark Johnson and Jamie Bloem in the Super League era. But there were also players who never made it after switching codes to play rugby league, and their stories are also told here.

Available for just £13.95 post free in the UK direct from London League Publications Ltd or from Amazon.co.uk . Credit card orders via www.llpshop.co.uk; payment by cheque to PO Box 65784, London NW2 9NS. Available in bookshops at £14.95.

Also available as an E-Book for Kindle from Amazon.

The Glory and the Dream is a great new rugby league novel. It tells the story of a young boy's rite of passage. It is full of rich characters, and is played out against a backdrop of social upheaval in the austere post-war years of rationing and shortages. But it was a time when communities pulled together. Walking days, royal visits, Sunday School outings to the seaside and communal bonfire nights were annual highlights. It was a time when youngsters had to make their own entertainment, including playing rugby league. It is about Johnny Gregson, the young star of the

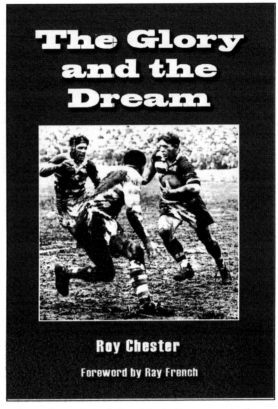

Garton rugby league team, whose dream is to follow his dad's success in the sport. Johnny lives with his mother in Four Locks, a poor working class area in a grimy northern town. His father died in the Second World War. The story starts in 1945, when Johnny is aged 10. It follows his rise from junior rugby league through playing rugby union as a schoolboy to turning professional with Garton.

Johnny faces challenges at every turn, including when he wins a scholarship to a local public school and is labelled as a 'slum kid;' by the class bully. His prowess at rugby helps him deal with this boy. Also, at the tender age of 16, he meets a young woman who becomes very important to him. This is a story about sport, romance and working class life. It includes many humorous incidents, insights and even tragedy in a young man's development.

Published in March 2014 at £9.95. Order for just £6.95 post free in the UK from www.llpshop.co.uk from London League Publications Ltd, PO Box 65784, London NW2 9NS

Also available as an E-Book for Kindle from Amazon.

Soldiers' League
The story of Army Rugby League
By Sean Fanning

"Rugby league epitomises all of the qualities required of a soldier – skill, fitness, courage, teamwork, determination and a strong sense of discipline."

Lieutenant General Sir Scott Grant, former President Army Rugby League.

Rugby league only became a recognised sport in the Army in 1994. However, since then it has thrived, overcoming many obstacles on the way. This book is the first to be published about rugby league in the Armed Forces. It covers the growth and development of the sport in the Army.

Sean Fanning played professional rugby league for Leigh and Highfield. He was a Staff Sergeant in the Army Medical Service until 2014, and was on active duty in Afghanistan in 2012. He has played for and coached the Army Rugby League team, played for the Great Britain Armed Forces team in the 2008 Armed Forces World Cup and has played for Combined Services. Sean Fanning's share of the profits from this book will be paid directly to Soldiers' League, which raises money for service charities, including the Royal British Legion, Blesma and Combat Stress.

Published in 2013 @ £14.95, now available direct from London League Publications Ltd at www.llpshop.co.uk for just £14.00 (£10 for current or former members of the Armed Forces) post free in the UK or by post from London League Publications Ltd, PO Box 65784, London NW2 9NS.

Also available as an E-Book for Kindle from Amazon.

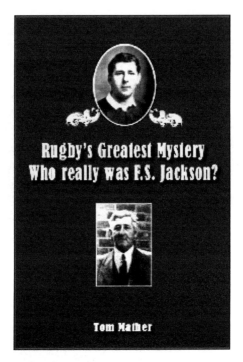

A true life rugby detective story

This is the story of a man whose life was made up of mystery, intrigue and deception, but was also a Rugby Union star before the First World War. He played for Leicester and Cornwall when they won the 1908 County Championship. He was selected for the Anglo-Welsh Rugby Union tour to New Zealand and Australia in 1908. However, the RFU recalled him from the tour and banned him from the sport over allegations that he was a professional player, and had played for Swinton in the Northern Union. The scandal around his suspension from rugby union caused great problems for the RFU and almost saw a further split in the game.

He then played rugby league for New Zealand, against the British Lions in 1910. After the First World War he was reinstated by the New Zealand RU, became an East Coast selector and saw his son play for the All Blacks. For around 60 years he used the name Frederick Stanley Jackson, even though it was not his given name. When he died in 1957 he took to the grave his true identity. Even his family knew little about his early years in England, or even where he came from. **It was a mystery that remained unresolved until now.** The book also includes an analysis of the development of Leicester Tigers RFC up to the First World War.

Published in March 2012 at £12.95. Special offer £6.95 post free in the UK available direct from London League Publications Ltd, PO Box 65784, London NW2 9NS (cheques payable to London League Publications Ltd)
credit card orders via our website: www.llpshop.co.uk or order from any bookshop.
Also available as an E-Book for Kindle from Amazon.

Braver than all the rest
A mother fights for her son

Philip Howard

Dave and Sarah Burgess are devastated when their young son Karl is found to have muscular dystrophy. Then another tragedy hits the family hard. But the family are committed to do the best they can for Karl, who has a passion for rugby league. Based in Castleton, a Yorkshire town near the border with Lancashire, Karl's determination to get the most out of life, despite his disability, inspires those around him, in particular Chris Anderton, one of the Castleton Rugby League Club players, who is coming to the end of his career in the game. A moving novel of family life and rugby league.

Published in 2010 at £9.95, special offer £7.00 post free in UK direct from London League Publications Ltd. Credit card orders via www.llpshop.co.uk orders by cheque to LLP, PO Box 65784, London NW2 9NS

Also available as an E-Book on Kindle for Amazon.

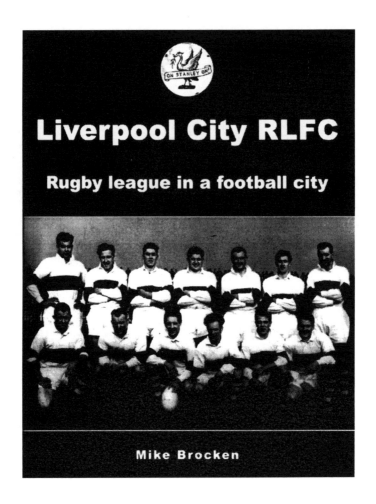

Liverpool City RLFC

Rugby league in a football city

Mike Brocken

The full story of rugby league in Liverpool from the sport's earliest days to the modern era.
Based on extensive research and interviews, a fascinating story of a struggle against the odds.

246 page paperback available direct from London League Publications Ltd for £14.95 post free in the UK. Visit www.llpshop.co.uk to order (credit cards via Pay Pal) or write to London League Publications Ltd, PO Box 65784 London NW2 9NS (cheques payable to London League Publications Ltd).

Also available as an E-Book for Kindle on Amazon.